Stop the Sabotage

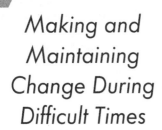

*Making and
Maintaining
Change During
Difficult Times*

HERMAN "RAY" BARBER

New York

Stop the Sabotage
Making and Maintaining Change During Difficult Times

HERMAN "RAY" BARBER

ISBN 978-1-61448-139-3 Paperback
ISBN 978-1-61448-140-9 eBook
Library of Congress Control Number: 2011938215

Published by:
Morgan James Publishing
The Entrepreneurial Publisher
5 Penn Plaza, 23rd Floor
New York City, New York 10001
(212) 655-5470 Office
(516) 908-4496 Fax
www.MorganJamesPublishing.com

Cover Design by:
Rachel Lopez
rachel@r2cdesign.com

Interior Design by:
Bonnie Bushman
bbushman@bresnan.net

In an effort to support local communities, raise awareness and funds, Morgan James Publishing donates one percent of all book sales for the life of each book to Habitat for Humanity. Get involved today, visit
www.HelpHabitatForHumanity.org.

Dedication

To Lynn— for her encouragement, love and support throughout our 20 years together.

Table of Contents

Introduction

Articles and books on the topic of change are as ubiquitous as fast food restaurants on the urban landscape. Changes that involve altering our attitude, motivation, and actions can allow us to move into better employment opportunities, relationships and a higher quality of life. Articles and books on weight loss and increasing health related behavior loom at us everywhere from the grocery store checkout line to the home pages of bookseller's websites. Thus the appeal of change is widely apparent.

Whether we are looking to improve our attitude, coping skills, income, relationships or any other facet of our life, most of us are not attempting this change for the first time. We have tried and we have failed. Repeated failures make future changes more difficult, and lower our expectations of ourselves. Like the cycle of poverty, the cycle of failing at changing ourselves can be self-perpetuating and overwhelming to break.

Stop the Sabotage differs from most because it explores the primary reasons why people don't succeed with making and then maintaining personal change. Personal sabotages stop us and we often have little insight as to why we fail. If these sabotages aren't recognized and addressed, the content of much self-help information is the equivalent of putting perfume on without ever taking a bath. If you have a lot of good self-help information stored from years of personal research, the content of *Stop the Sabotage* may allow it to finally work for you. In many ways, the first chapters of *Stop the Sabotage* are analogous to taking a bath to rid you of layers of dirt in the form of personal sabotages.

Stop the Sabotage is for anyone that struggles with making and maintaining change. It is also for those who teach change principles that are inspirational, motivational, and spiritual but who have somehow lost their way in a sea of theoretical principles. Here you have a concrete and systematic process to guide you to achieve and then maintain your goals.

Use *Stop the Sabotage* as a workbook. One problem with the information age is that we can access too much information without being challenged to think critically and creatively. The purpose of *Stop the Sabotage* is to gain personal clarity. However, it is important to realize that this text was not written to focus on hypothetical situations with which others struggle. *Stop the Sabotage* isn't a novel or a biography. *Stop the Sabotage* is about and for you.

Clarity will come when you make sure you understand each point before moving on to the next. With each point, ask yourself how this relates to you. I cannot connect all of your dots; this is your job in your search for reason and understanding. It is necessary for you to make and to maintain change.

I have spent most of the past 30 years working with people served by non-profit and public human services. I also teach parenting skills as a volunteer in a homeless shelter. Thus, I have a frame of reference for people who really struggle without the benefit of a decent income, health insurance or support networks. I take your feelings and your struggles very seriously and I don't have any vested interests in selling you fantasies and theories.

Let us now begin with eliminating those sabotages that have kept you from moving forward with life. This will be an adventure—a journey towards both knowing yourself better, realizing your strengths and removing any roadblocks to making and maintaining change.

Discounting
Information

Where do we begin in our increasingly important quest to make and to maintain change? With the advent of the information age, we can access information with a few strokes on the keyboard, watch an on-line video or listen to discussion about the topic of change. Thus, the quantity of information isn't at issue and much of the available information is excellent. However, we seem to be stuck. My opinion is that people increasingly discount perfectly good information.

In selecting the order of *Stop the Sabotage*, I placed discounting information at the beginning because this can sabotage the utilization of the remainder of the book and all self-help information. Unfortunately discounting information is one of the major reasons why people do not benefit from therapy, self-help books, CDs, podcasts, talk shows and many other sources of good information that could be helpful in making life changes.

Those who discount educational and self-help information often impose the supposition that, unless the information is perfectly aligned with their personal beliefs and their exact circumstances, it is flawed information and thus could not possibly be useful. This is a common excuse for not moving forward. This reasoning also feeds our need to be terminally unique.

If you are reading *Stop the Sabotage*, evidently your methods of trying to make and maintain change have not been totally successful. Thus you must not have the answers and/or the motivation to do it on your own. Tell yourself that you will read *Stop the Sabotage* with an open mind and without spending time and energy pointing out things with which you don't agree. This advice will put you on the right track and will serve as a long-term life lesson. Finding and using good information that works for you isn't some sort of reality show where you are voting people off an island. In the world of making and maintaining personal change, you are the biggest loser when you become too judgmental about self-help information.

If someone is really striving to make lasting change, lessons can be found anywhere and from anyone. Many of the lessons found in *Stop the Sabotage* have been derived from those who had problems with segments of their lives, but who also had areas of great insight, wisdom and success.

If you wish to learn acting techniques, would you listen to an award-winning actor who had problems with infidelity or drug addiction? If you are a talented singer, would you take advice about singing from someone with three Grammy Awards but who had problems with personal relationships? Great actors, singers, athletes and politicians often have noticeable character flaws, but they know their area of expertise and have a great deal to teach.

Take a look back at your own history and select some of the most profound lessons that have stuck with you. Did these lessons come from perfect people or perfect events? We may find perfection in one area of a person's life and may consider them a role model. But people we admire for certain strengths often have imperfections. A great deal of our current media is built around pointing out people's flaws and shortcomings. We are exposed to an on-going barrage of invitations to discredit others. This often leads us to discount excellent information because we are becoming much too cynical.

Can you name a few professional athletes and movie stars that, although experts in their profession have fallen into some serious problems of their own making? Hopefully you don't discount the importance of their contributions because of imperfections. If you struggle with discounting people and thus their lessons, make an effort to get past their imperfections. Looking at the imperfections of others is a way of not looking at yourself and your own imperfections.

During my first two years of graduate school, I worked in a therapeutic community for the treatment of drug addiction. This community consisted of mostly heroin addicts and many were very adept at using their defenses to fend off any sort of change. One common problem among people in long-term substance abuse treatment is that they will look for faults in the staff so that they don't have to look at their own issues. Their magical thinking was that they would not have to change unless the staff members were paragons of virtue. Thus a focus of treatment was to teach the residents that taking stock of other people's imperfections was not going to help them become drug-free, happy and productive.

As children we all learn how to best control our environment so to maintain as much comfort as possible. Children often learn the skill of refocusing attention away from themselves and onto others. When confronting these children they quickly point out any imperfections in the adult. Discrediting others is a common defense against change and is often perfected with age as we begin building our ego—that part of us that we totally construct. Discounting the ideas of others is an inherent part of the process of internally defending against change.

Tabloid news is a classic example of media that discounts others. Tabloid news is a paradise for those who enjoy keeping the focus on others while not spending time and effort in self-improvement activities. It appears that when we get overly focused on Tiger Wood, Al Gore, or others who have made errors in judgment, we tend to spend less time looking at ourselves.

Take a moment to look at the ways that you have traditionally discounted information that may have been helpful? Do you find yourself increasingly looking at the misfortunes of others to realize how well you are doing? If you are overweight, do you tend to focus on those who have a much more severe weight problem or those are too underweight to really be healthy? As you confront yourself with such questions, are you also saying "yes, but?"

I have known many people who say "yes, but" to every piece of advice. Some seem to be looking for an exact prescription for their special problems, however they will take prescription medication that was not specifically designed and manufactured for their exact physical problem. One useful exercise is to be aware of each time that you say "yes, but". Once you become aware of saying these words think about why you are saying them. The utterance of these words is often a symptom of "terminal uniqueness".

Terminal uniqueness is one of the biggest excuses for discounting useful information. It means you believe your problem or situation is very different from those that other people experience. If you truly believe this, do a bit of reality testing. To some, being terminally unique makes them special and we all love to feel special. There is secondary gain in feeling special. If we feel special by feeling that our problems are unique, then this can become part of our self-identity. Do you want your problems and excuses to be part of how others define you and how you define yourself? Self-indulgence in feeling crappy about yourself can become a way of life that isn't really going to allow self-improvement into your life.

Besides attitudes and self-images that hinder growth, there are a number of issues that are hard-wired into our psyche. At times, simple awareness of these processes will allow us to recognize why we are getting off the track with personal change. With this awareness, we can slowly and intentionally move forward.

During the time that I taught introductory psychology, students seemed to love the chapters on sensation and perception. They were fascinated about how the human brain often fills-in missing pieces of information. For example, the missing letters in a neon sign are hardly noticed because we fill in the blanks. We also tend to correct stimuli in our environment that is not correct. There are many example of this phenomenon.

When I primarily treated clients with post-traumatic stress disorder and dissociative identity disorder (multiple personality disorder), I took some classes on the topic of psycholinguistics. This gave me a different view of how the human brain will tarnish and discount information or change the thought process. An example will clarify my point.

If I am in the early stage of working with a rape victim and exploring her personal story of rape and the accompanying feelings,

I will simply listen to the story. She may say that the five-foot eight, blue eyed, blonde man approached her in a dark blue Ford pick-up truck. She may then state many details about his appearance and manner. However, when I paraphrase her words back to her, I should speak in generalities. "When the man approached you there, then, and that happened, what were you feeling?" If I attempt to repeat her exact words and made a mistake in any of the details, she would most likely get out of her feelings and into her thoughts in order to correct me. For example, if I said that the man was in a light blue Ford van, this would typically stop the flow of feelings and she would correct me. The lesson in this story is that we tend to pick-out details from information that aren't exactly correct. The next step is often to discount the information.

In this example, one can see that we tend to listen to someone very closely until we find ourselves verbally or non-verbally correcting his or her inaccuracies. This is a form of discounting information. To make this point, I kept a few writing errors in *Stop the Sabotage*. See how quickly you can move past these while staying focused on the message and not the error.

The paradox in this process is that we tend to pick-out the details from information that isn't exactly correct—as we know them to be correct. If we are and have been looking for resolution for our personal change agenda, we evidently don't know all of the answers. We only know what we know. This is one of many reasons to digest self-help information with a very open mind.

During a conversation, don't stop and correct someone who makes a simple mistake. While reading material, don't correct every mistake or think about how it could have been written better—unless you are being paid as an editor. If an article has one flaw or inaccuracy, don't focus just on that part. After years of practice, I can hear more of what is being said to me and I retain much more of the material that I see, hear and experience.

One secondary gain from this type of exercise is that you will learn the true answer to the meaning of the question "would I rather be right or would I rather be happy?" Would I rather be critical or kind? Is your ego so fragile that your self-esteem varies from high to low depending on whether you are right or wrong? Are you one who looks for deficits rather than for strengths?

When we are shopping for information for our own personal benefit, we need to turn down mechanisms that discount incoming information. There is a saying in group therapy and 12-step programs that we should use what fits and discard the rest. This is excellent advice but I recommend taking it one step further. I often believe that things we hear today may be useful later in life. For that reason it is good to use what fits today and store the remainder for another day.

I discuss this point in parenting classes. I frequently hear testimonials from parents about lessons that their parents and others taught them as children. Although they discounted this information at the time, later in life they recognized the value of the early lessons and used this information to their benefit. Perhaps you have your own examples of how this applies to you.

Why do people take one small piece of information and discount all of it? Although this may be intellectual dogmatism, this is frequently derived from fear of being incorrect about old ideas. People do not like to admit that they are wrong. Before we will admit that we are wrong, we will reinforce our old stance and defend it. It is one thing to do this in public to save face, but information that comes to you in the privacy of your own space can be agreed upon without admitting anything to others. As children, we learn not to believe everything we read, as mature adults we learn not to believe everything we initially think.

As adults, many of us learn that listening to our ego is pretty much a joke. As we realize that our ego is a construct of our own making, we learn to get further and further from it and the garbage it brings to contaminate our lives. If I find myself in a space where my ego seems to be running my life, I think of something for which I am grateful. Since the ego and gratitude can't occupy the same space, I quickly find myself centered in a healthy place.

Many people get caught-up in the trap of monolithic thinking. This practice is common among those who propose that, unless we agree with their rhetoric, we are BAD. Bad is a relative word that in recent years may imply that one is un-American, un-patriotic or un-Christian. Those who polarize society require that we all take sides. People on each side of an issue have their own particular beliefs. We often believe that we are expected to agree with 100 percent of a group's beliefs or not at all. This supposition makes it uncomfortable for many of us to pick and choose our beliefs individually rather than selecting entire ideologies. We then generalize this to self-help information.

When we look at our personal philosophy or ideology, there are those who are like us and those who are not like us. Those like us are often framed as good and those not like us are framed as not so good. Thus we often tend to listen to those who are like us. If we don't know anything about the person or organization that is offering us new information, we are looking for clues as to whether they are like us or fall into the camp of those who are not like us.

Areas such as politics and religion are two of the great areas of differentiation. The point here is that people who don't think as we think and who don't subscribe to our belief systems can offer excellent information. Do you know the religious and political affiliation of your doctor, dentist or attorney? If so, why should you care?

When we look for clues as to whether a person is like us, we tend to search for signs of commonality or difference. In the process we seldom hear the entire message. When reading material that contains useful personal information, avoid the tendency to determine whether the presenter of the information is like or not like you.

Another underlying belief and practice that feeds the process of discounting information is that a person may not be comfortable with picking and choosing bits and pieces of information to arrive at a solution. Fear of what others will think can be a major roadblock. Fear that you will identify yourself with those "other people" can also stop us in our tracks.

Think about the world of information as a grocery, clothing or furniture store. Do you always buy prepared meals from a box or from the freezer? Many of us will put together a meal by combining various types of foods. We mix and match. We buy meat that we can serve with different pasta and vegetables. In putting together a wardrobe, we buy a shirt or blouse that will go with different pants and skirts. In decorating a room, we often combine color, form, and texture to fit our taste. Much of the content of *Stop the Sabotage* is about variety and about picking those things that fit your individual needs.

I taught Transitional Analysis® (TA) for many years. From the perspective of TA®, some people will select an "I'm OK—You're not OK" life position because they don't feel good about themselves—not because they feel superior. I often used Archie Bunker as a good example of someone who takes this life position. During the early years of the television series All in the Family, Archie put people down because he did not feel good about himself. He discounted blacks, Jews, intellectuals and many others because he had a dead-end job and a very limited education and understanding about the world in which he lived.

Anyone who is dogmatic in his or her thinking will discount perfectly good ideas because there is a small piece of the idea that does not fit into his or her worldview. Hatred for a person or a group can sabotage one's efforts to change. Believing that only those who believe as you believe can keep you stuck in a sea of ignorance and bigotry.

I recall developing my first co-existing world-view during elementary school. I recall the day that I was introduced to the scientific method. I immediately had a revelation that science and the scientific method were not the end-all in knowledge and reason. Upon learning the scientific method, I immediately knew that it was an extremely important tool on the continuum of methods of knowing information. I believe in it, use it, teach it; but I know there is much more in the universe than the scientific method can ever explain or prove.

Quantum physics clarifies that we can neither explain nor predict some events and processes with certainty. Thus I am open to spiritual teachings, lessons from the arts, or from those who know nothing of science. Answers can be found in some of the most unlikely places. Because you believe in one thing doesn't necessarily mean that you are opposed to something else.

Social psychologists have much to teach about why we tend to discount or discredit concepts and ideas. For example, we tend to believe in what we do (i.e. our profession and religion). We may especially believe in things that we have suffered for. If most people living in a particular geographic area work in the defense industry, they will more likely have strong opinions in favor of defense spending. People have strong opinions about those things that contribute to and preserve a high standard of living. Parents of school age children generally have stronger opinions about educational issues and the elderly have stronger opinions of issues that benefit them. This all may seem overly simplistic, but knowing why we believe in something can clarify why we blemish the ideas of others.

One summer I took a course in urban sociology. On the first day of class, each student had to pull a number of identities out of a hat. We randomly selected our age, race, sex, income, marital status, number of children, and the location of our home in the city. I remember one male student complaining that he was a single woman with three children. He wanted to know if he was divorced or whether he had ever been married. During the summer we voted on all sorts of town issues including the placement of roads, the budget, and the need for various public services. The more the incongruity between a person's real identity and their identity for this class, the more the student learned.

When we discount ideas we often paint ourselves into a corner. Exploration of why we discount ideas, that we either do not understand or that which we do not agree, can allow us to greatly broaden our worldview. Carte blanche acceptance is not the opposite of discounting ideas. Having an open mind and not quickly drawing hasty conclusions are laudable goals.

Sometimes we find that discounting ideas is simply a matter of saying that we are not really ready to change. This is honest and this stance can be revisited later in life. Change can be difficult and maintaining change may be overwhelming—especially after numerous attempts. However read on to find a method that you can claim as yours—a method that will work for you.

A very wise mentor stated to me early in my career, "Don't take something from someone unless you offer something to replace it." With that in mind, *Stop the Sabotage* will suggest alternatives to replacing those practices, thoughts, and feelings that you choose to discard.

2   Structuring Time

When people don't achieve their goals many will say that they just didn't have enough time. There are many observable ironies regarding both the availability and the utilization of time. For example people say that they don't have time to exercise. However they will spend inordinate amounts of time watching TV, surfing the web, talking on the phone, and participating in other activities that don't produce positive outcomes. Exercise isn't an either/or proposition as one can talk on the phone, watch a video, dictate into a computer, and perform many other tasks while exercising.

With the high unemployment rate the unemployed especially grapple with the best use of time. Although finding employment is a key goal, leaning new skills is equally important. For example if one owns a computer, down time from work is a time to learn how to touch type and how to efficiently use software such as Microsoft Office. The effective use of time can easily make the difference in succeeding with your life goals.

There are many ways in which we structure our time. We structure our time on two levels. The first level is how we physically spend our time. Our day may include eight hours of working in our profession, two hours of reading during our commute, an hour of meal preparation and eating. We may spend some time watching TV, going to the gym and helping children with homework.

I recommend periodically evaluating how you physically spend your time. This little evaluative exercise allows us to inventory our use of time and to make changes in our priorities. There is a lot of good material available on the topic of time management. If this is something that you wish to improve upon, attend a good time management course or purchase an audio program on this topic. Many of the planning systems that include calendars, priority setting tools, goal setting, and tracking sheets will get you off to a fast start on planning your time more wisely.

Some people are always searching for that perfect time management system and spend time and money each year on a new type of system. If a time management system doesn't seem to work despite your best efforts, you may find the remainder of this chapter particularly interesting because it could explain why these systems haven't made an appreciable difference in your life. If your goal is to do more with the time that you have available, you may have issues with managing your mental time.

Other goals for improved time management can have very different outcomes. One possible outcome may be to feel less stressed. A goal of time management may be to have increased happiness and serenity—often by doing less. Often people say that they wish to be more efficient rather than to accomplish more.

If you have used one or more methods to improve your time management but continue to struggle, perhaps you should look for some clues regarding your use of mental time. A focus on our mental structuring of time is an unconventional method of looking at time management. Our mental structuring of time often seems to be more capricious and out of our control. We often do not consider those processes that occur between our ears to be as intentional or controlled as those things that physically occupy our time. The structuring of our mental time may be very different than that of our physical structure of time.

Many of the things that physically occupy our time do not require our full concentration. We physically complete many tasks that do not require our complete concentration. You can say that, when you are doing one thing and thinking about something else, your brain is multi-tasking. The recent focus on the problems caused by people texting while driving indicates how far we will go to multi-task when we should be concentrating on one activity.

Unless you have mastered meditative states where you can clear your mind, you are always thinking during your waking hours. Much of the time you are not solely thinking about what you are doing. Tomorrow, be aware of how much of your time is spent completely concentrating on the task at hand.

I have taken a daily inventory of my thoughts and have found that my mind wanders all over the place. My wife will tell me about her day at the clinic and I will think about how this relates to other things, such as what I said to a consumer and whether my granddaughter has begun talking and, if so, what she said. While working out at the gym, I think about whatever seems to be of primary concern for that day until I intermittently begin thinking about the people in the gym. Often I watch a movie in the upper left corner of my computer, work on the computer and think about many things at the same time.

People can go to work, perform their duties and obsess about things that may or may not be job related. As you can see, our physical and mental structure of time can be very different while often occurring simultaneously.

What is your personal frame of reference for doing one thing while thinking about something entirely different? We can cross over a line when our use of mental time interferes with our ability to accomplish our goals. There are clues when we need to reign-in our use of mental time. One indication may be your ability to actively listen to others. Most of us spend a great deal of time listening to others either in person or through some other form of communication. Self-centeredness, as exhibited by problems with being attentive to others, can block one's abilities to structure time.

There is also active and passive listening. In active listening, you really hear the content of what others tell you. The passive listener doesn't hear a great deal of what is said and retains even less. I have noted a positive correlation between a person's difficulty with structuring their mental time and their ability to actively listen. Active listening requires a certain level of attentiveness to another person and thus requires that one's thoughts must not be scattered among a sea of second-guessing and anticipatory thoughts. For some, active listening is a unique experience and is not part of everyday life. Others find active listening to be second nature.

The development of active listening as an exercise to focus on something external is a practice in self-discipline and an incremental step toward controlling one's focus and thoughts. Intentional listening is a skill that, once developed, can allow one to utilize sources of information that were referenced in the last chapter. With practice we can learn much from the simplest of conversations regardless of the speaker's education, life experience and character flaws.

Rumination and obsession are thought processes, compulsions are behaviors, and addictions can be manifestations of the two that can involve physical predispositions. For the purpose of this discussion, I will focus on obsessive thinking. Many people report sleepless nights when their mind cannot seem to break away from a particular topic. I remember staying awake during high school as I fixated on lecturing a large auditorium of people about matters of social justice. As I entered the world of work, marriage and parenthood, the topics changed, but I continued this practice well into my 40s.

Obsessing is not limited to nighttime or to solitary moments. Many of us ruminate and obsess quite well during those times spent out of bed and with others. One of the most well known obsessive statements is "why did he or she do that?" We can spend a great deal of time trying to figure out why people believe and behave the way they do. For example, during election years members of one political party may obsess about how those from the opposing party could possibly think differently than they think. If this obsessive thinking is related to one's job, this works, makes money and fills a social niche. However, this often isn't the case.

Obsessions fall into an area that I have already mentioned— things that we cannot change. Social injustice, stories of devastating events and many other topics can put us into a loop of thoughts and emotions that go on for extended periods of time. Obsessive thinking truly sabotages our ability to structure our time and to be productive. If we are simultaneously trying to make a change in our life, obsessive thinking robs us of the time and energy to focus on making and maintaining change.

So as not to minimize certain conditions, obsessive thinking that is due to personal trauma is quite different from the obsessing that most people do. Trauma based obsessions can change our biology and recovery may require the assistance of a mental health professional.

Some will argue that the structuring of mental time is not a choice and that we cannot control where our thoughts take us. I argue that the structuring of our mental time is a choice for the majority of us. With awareness and practice we can change how we structure our mental time. It is our thoughts that lead us more than our biology. It is the content of our thoughts that determine where we take our lives and ultimately determine who we become.

Be aware of your thoughts for one weekday and one day during the weekend. Record your discoveries in a journal and review this journal on a regular basis. Be particularly aware of the percentage of your thoughts that are about those things that you cannot change. If most of your thoughts fall into this category, you have a serious problem if you are working toward making a personal change. The slow and intentional process of replacing wasted thoughts with productive ones is a bit challenging because unproductive thinking is an activity that becomes part of our structure of time.

When you remove something from your typical structure of mental time, you should replace it with something else. If you could totally stop your unproductive thoughts you would need to replace them with something. If not, there would be a void in your life. How would you fill this void?

Develop a few inspirational thoughts about positive endeavors that you would like to pursue. Use your imagination to picture yourself achieving your goals, accomplishing a task, or enjoying the benefits of personal accomplishment. These are topics to be discussed in later chapters, but now is the time to recognize the significance of structuring your mental time.

After taking these steps, go further by then focusing on how you can assist others. Think about how wonderful it would be to want what you want for yourself more for others. Ponder the importance of letting go of your ego and responding with kindness and love toward others, instead of holding on to the hatred, resentment and personal comparisons with others.

Motivational material frequently states that we are in control of our attitude. Much of our attitude is based on well-developed belief systems. For some, attitude adjustment is a small step. For others, it is a giant leap away from a long history of non-productive thinking. For those who have distance to travel in the development of a positive attitude, there are many useful methods.

There is an old statement in substance abuse treatment programs that suggests that you "fake it until you make it." Stated another way, you can "act as if" you totally believe that you will change and, with this behavioral change, there will come an improved attitude. If you practice saying good morning to people and being friendly, your feelings will eventually catch on. If you put a sticky note on your bathroom mirror that says, "You are in charge of your attitude today!" you will eventually realize that this is true and that others do not make you have negative feelings.

Through working on increasing your motivation and improving your attitude, you can structure your mental time in such a way that change can occur. This in turn will make further changes much easier. There is a great deal of motivational material available in every format. Remember that motivational material must be omnipresent in our lives.

One paradox about time is that the less we have to do, the less time we have to do it. I have heard this statement most of my life. It became real to me in high school when I would procrastinate about homework and study. I had little to do but study; however, I would never seem to have enough time. Some of the most hurried people that I know have very little to do. They pack their lives with fluff in order to feel busy and, most significantly, to feel important.

Keep in mind that you go where your thoughts take you. If you think about what you don't have, you will manifest more of what you don't have. We manifest those things that we think about. If you spend much of your time thinking about things that you cannot change and the helplessness, hopelessness and confusion that accompany these thoughts, you cannot expect to mentally go to a better place. Think about those who frequently think about how awful things are and whether they seem to advance their lives in positive ways. Those who are focused, intentional and enlightened are present for themselves and others and live in the now.

Part of structuring time is structuring time for leisure. Leisure is a relative concept that is based on many factors. What some people consider leisure, others may see as work. I believe that leisure activities are those things in which we entirely lose the concept of time. True leisure takes me to a mental place where time can pass and I haven't a clue as to how long I have been involved in the activity. While in this mental space I don't think about work or upcoming projects or problems.

A few questions to ponder include the following:

- How do you define leisure?
- Does it take you to another place in your mind?
- How easy is it to replicate this feeling?

- Must you physically be in a particular type of
  environment to experience true leisure?

Leisure time is an excellent opportunity to use your imagination to augment your ability to get outside of yourself. If you are a reader, you can allow yourself an opportunity to put yourself into some of the characters, places and events—as long as these choices give you comfort. I sometimes sit on my upper deck and watch the planes fly over and think of all the places the passengers have been or are going. I will pick a place and mentally go there. Using our imagination is a wonderful activity. Allow yourself time to slip into the leisurely bliss of your imagination.

There is a common saying that goes something like this: "how can you expect something different when you keep doing the same thing that you have always done?" The answer is that you really shouldn't. If you spend your mental time finding fault in others, thinking about how bad things have gotten and how you wish the good old days would return, how could you expect anything different from what you have? Those who find themselves stuck in life may benefit from asking themselves this question on a daily basis.

One final thought is to again look at the concept of knowing what you can change and what you cannot. This is a focus of the next chapter. I could spend the entire day thinking about things I cannot control. I could find others who would be willing to spend inordinate amounts of time talking about how awful some things are and they would not have any more control over these events than I have.

The growth of the tabloid media feeds our need to spend time ruminating about negative events and events that we cannot change. One change that can be a prerequisite for making other changes is to limit the amount of time that you watch the news and those programs that focus on how awful people and events can be. If the structuring of mental time is a problem and you tend to ruminate on bad news, don't feed the problem with large doses of negative information.

While teaching human development in graduate school, I recall stating that teens fall on the rung of social ladders based on their ability to fit comfortably within social groups. They gravitate to a comfort zone of peers. Although they may aspire to a higher rung on the ladder they often do not wish to take the risk to move up. Unfortunately, people become fixed at this comfort level and stay there the remainder of their life. I know 35-year-old males who live in a world of video games and make believe characters. Although they work, pay bills and survive, they seem to lack the ability to move forward despite their statements indicating the desire to "get out of the rut." This is a "structure of time" issue that relates to personal history and to comfort level.

Sometimes it is important to understand how you got to be where you are. Much of psychotherapy is based on re-deciding old decisions. Most old decisions were good decisions within the context of the person-in-situation environment and the time and circumstances in which they were made. However, old decisions can be re-decided once they are found to no longer work. See if some re-decisions would assist you in structuring your time.

You will discern some overlap between this chapter and the next because mentally cleaning out unproductive thoughts has a direct relationship with the ability to save and to reinvest mental time.

3

Throwing Out the Garbage

Before self-help books, CDs, podcasts, TV talk shows and therapy will assist you and maintaining your desired change, you need to clear your mind of thoughts that rob you of the ability to progress. With the advent of the information age we now have endless options for acquiring information. Websites, blogs, social networking sites and other web-based options have added layers to the plethora of information that we can access.

There has been a real revival in recent years of the belief that our thoughts guide our lives. This idea is centuries old, but yet has been resurrected. When our thoughts have accompanying positive emotion, we can fully utilize our internal abilities to change our lives. Whether one adheres to this belief or not, most would agree that it is more beneficial for each of us to think positively about self and others than to be filled with cynicism and disgust. The realization that our thoughts and feelings is a choice for most of us can be a major step toward making and maintaining change.

I have been an ACE Certified Personal Training and NSPA Certified Conditioning Specialist since 1994 and I often use wellness analogies. For example, someone who consumes large amounts of fast food, sodas containing sugar, and junk food is filling their bodies with garbage that will eventually take its toll. The garbage with which we fill our minds isn't all that different.

Some people put themselves on a diet of bad news but I do not believe they plan to do this. Bad news becomes entertainment and, in some strange sense, makes us feel one-up on others. Focusing on other people, places, and events may keep us full, but with toxic waste. We are surrounded by examples of how misery and disgust enter our lives. As stated in chapter one, "Discounting Information," we began looking at how the dynamics of looking for imperfections in others can cause us to discount perfectly useful information.

My car dealer gave me a loaner because my car required some engine work. The radio was on a station that I had never heard. At first I thought that this call-in talk show was the radio equivalent of Saturday Night Live. After about 10 minutes I realized that those speaking weren't actors trying to be funny by saying hateful and disgusting things, but it was actually a serious discussion. I then realized that, because this was a commercial station, this type of program must make money from those who loved to talk hate and who fed off being bitter, fearful and disgusted with life. I had been introduced to this type of problem from a very different perspective about 40 years ago.

An old friend of mine grew-up in the Watts section of Los Angeles. He once related that he never watched movies or TV shows about such topics as drugs, prostitution, and violent crime. When he was growing up he frequently saw these acts and knew what people were capable of doing to one another and to themselves. His point was that once he knew about these things he didn't really need an ongoing dose of the same reality. Seeing what people are capable of doing doesn't really change the reality and tends to make one cynical, disgusted and fearful. Fear is often the result of too many reminders of social issues of which we are well aware, but which we cannot easily change.

My grandmother always said that fear and God cannot occupy the same space. However, she said this before my family owned a TV. As society increases its voyeuristic activities into the lives of others, the potential for a fear-based life increases. People do peculiar things when they are fearful and fear shapes the ego in ways that perpetuates many of the issues that causes the fear.

If one is fearful of a minority group, he or she will often adopt many fear-based attitudes and beliefs. Fearful people band together to justify, rationalize, and intellectualize why we all should be fearful and then try to take us to a place of fear. We can suddenly find ourselves back at the crossroads of determining whether people are like us or not like us. If they are not enough like us, we are likely to dislike and fear them.

The process of cleaning out the thought garbage is like cleaning out a cluttered basement, attic, or hard drive. There should be a reason why we keep things. Have we used something within the past year? If we think that someone will want an item when we die, can we give it to him or her now? Do you want your children, grandchildren or strangers going through all of your belongings after you are dead and deciding whether an item can bring a few dollars at a yard sale, should be donated or thrown in the garbage?

Although we will all leave stuff behind, hopefully it will be those things with some utilitarian value and that someone can easily give away or trash. If we have sentimental items, perhaps we have family or friends willing to take these because they will be special. The secret is to continually inventory your property as well as your thoughts so that you aren't using valuable space to house useless junk.

How do we begin to throw out the garbage in our minds? If you are paying close attention, you may have guessed. The logical place to begin is to toss out all of those thoughts about the things you cannot change. Simply by listening to what other people talk about, I realize that many people primarily think about things they cannot change. We can play the blame game about why the economy is in the tank and who caused what, but can you change the big picture?

Listen to a phone conversation or a conversation in a restaurant. For example, our opinions about other people are sometimes very lengthy and detailed, but we cannot change those people. However, it does serve the purpose of keeping a conversation going and everyone does this to some extent. The key here is to take a close look at what you are thinking outside the realm of conversation.

Let us begin with thoughts about people that we really do not like—perhaps those with whom we don't agree. How many of your thoughts are about them? Can you change these people? I don't think so. People with opposing political, religious, and social views can eat away a lot of your thought space, time and serenity.

Don't spend time thinking about things you are not going to do. This can occupy quite a chunk of space. If you think about the jobs you aren't going to do and why you aren't going to do them, you are filing your mental space with empty boxes. However positive thoughts about what you are going to do and how you plan to do them is an excellent use of space.

Spending a lot of time thinking about how you don't want to be like a particular person in the news and how you could not possibly share their views does not change anything. They don't care what you think and dwelling over things you are not going to do or think is a total waste of time. People read tabloid news and watch tabloid TV and become upset about other people who have some celebrity status. Being an actor, singer, or pro-sports star doesn't teach people how to cope with life any better than someone who works at a factory, restaurant or a store.

Thoughts that are creative, loving, inspiring, and generally make you and the world a better place to live have a cumulative effect on you and on others. Just imagine if everyone had less hate and more love and compassion. Match your positive thoughts to the importance of recycling efforts; every can, bottle, piece of paper and plastic container that you recycle makes a difference.

Most people can easily fill many large garbage bags with all the thoughts that feed their ego. Thoughts about what you need can go first. Most of these thoughts are fillers. If you could really have all you think you need, you would not have any place to put it. Besides you are doing without these things now so evidently you do not need them. Get real with yourself about what you want versus what you need.

Realize that most of the truly happy people in the world do not define themselves by what they own. All of your thoughts about how others will perceive you differently if you only had X, Y, and

Z may be true, but why would you wish for others to perceive you differently? This will be discussed more fully in chapter 6.

A great place to begin to clean house and free up space, time and energy is to reduce your thoughts and ideas about those things with which you disagree, but cannot change. Ideas about religion, politics, and workplace gossip come to mind. Unlike the problem noted previously, these ideas are not necessarily attached to a particular person. It is one thing to have a brief conversation about topics over which you disagree and then move on, but we all know people who ruminate on these topics.

Often the thoughts come in the form of the question that I mentioned earlier, "Why do people believe and do the things they do?" You cannot change why someone thinks the way they think, nor can you change their accompanying behavior. As a therapist, I have influenced people to make changes that they wanted to make, but I didn't change them. They changed themselves. Also, people have the right to believe what they choose to believe.

There is a limit to the usefulness of providing someone with additional information. People's desire to learn more about a topic is often based on whether they are perfectly happy about what they know about a particular topic. For example, I could learn more about personal training, but I am pleased with the amount of information that I currently have. Outside of earning continuing education credits every two years for re-accreditation, I don't want to know more. More information isn't always the answer unless what you know isn't working for you to accomplish your personal goals.

We can neither commit troops to fight in another country, nor can we withdraw them once they are there. I personally know people who continue to ruminate over the second war in Iraq and the subsequent events. Others are constantly focused on the downturn in the economy and have been paralyzed by their thoughts.

Some people will use the other popular, but old-fashioned term for obsessing —they worry. Worry is a great term that is interpreted in many different ways. Some people believe that when one person truly worries about another person it is a sign of love and concern. Some believe that worry serves a purpose and is an obligation. Other people believe that it is a cultural trait.

There is not any magic that occurs as a result of worrying. If people tell me that they are worried about me going to Miami during the hurricane season and I believe that they really will worry, I do not respond. I just do not feed this obsession. The people doing the worrying are taking up time and mental energy for something that they do not have any control over and the worry is not going to prove useful to me if a hurricane occurs. Worry is totally useless on both ends.

Worry can net some real world results: one can develop ulcers and other stress-related problems. These will naturally provide other things to worry about. Some people binge-eat while others begin building resentments when they cannot change the person that they are worrying about. Some people identify themselves as worriers. This can be a role within the family. You may have even heard people say something like, "Aunt Sarah is the family worrier; she can do the worrying for everyone." Those on the receiving end of worry can feel guilty, apologetic, or resentful. Worry can eat up a lot of useful mental time and space.

There are those of us who love to obsess about causes. It is good to have a cause if one takes an active role in promoting the cause.

Some of my volunteer activities include teaching parenting skills in a homeless shelter and reviewing human services agencies for an accrediting organization. These activities relate to areas where I have concerns—homelessness, and the quality of human services. If you are for or against a cause, then do something rather than expending valuable mental energy and time thinking or worrying about it.

One great rule of thumb that is 100 percent accurate is you cannot change the past. If you are thinking about a person, place, or event that occurred in the past, you know that you cannot change it. Thinking of the good things that happened in our past can be a rewarding and inspirational way to pass some of our time. However, we can also obsess about the good things to the point that this stops us from moving on. If obsessive memories are related to grief, it is often a good idea to use a mental health professional or a support group to help us grieve and then move on.

However, the more common problem is spending our mental energy thinking about bad things that lie in the past. Think of those things that occurred in the past as exactly what they are—historic events. This has helped me to see that I cannot change history. In one sense things that occurred yesterday are as much part of history as those things that occurred before you were born. You cannot turn back the clock and change them. You can make current choices based on historical events. If you had a really negative experience with a person, place, thing, or event, you can make decisions about how to avoid this negative experience from occurring again. If last night's date was a total loser, you don't have to go out with that person again.

All news is old news. Look at how much of the news, especially the sensationalist variety, moves us to determine how bad people can be. It is as if we need a daily dose of people's mean, and cruel, acts against others. After watching this, it would be quite easy to assume that most things that happen are negative. When this is the case, our mind will gravitate toward negative thoughts when we aren't busy. One misfortune about 24-hour news channels is that people obsessively watch them and then become paranoid about crime, natural disasters, and slowly move toward misanthropy.

Also, there is obsessing over the future. Most of us do not have a clue about how we would react if we lost everything and had to live in a homeless shelter. There are countless scenarios that could occur each day, yet people will ruminate about the future. They will go on and on about a catalog of "what ifs": sudden unemployment, unexpected disease, or a transfer to another city.

Worrying about the future and planning for the future are two entirely different things. If someone plans so that they are employable in at least two careers, takes care of their health, and invests wisely for their future; they are less likely to worry. However, we cannot make contingency plans for everything that could go wrong in life. We can adopt an attitude that whatever happens to us has the potential to be the best thing that can happen.

Much of the garbage that we need to discard is related to guilt. Most guilt is about the past. While working as the Clinical Coordinator for the US Department of Veteran's Affairs I was forced to look at this issue. Quite of few of my clients were working on resolving issues of guilt. Much of this guilt was survivor's guilt. When guilt is this embedded over such serious issues, therapy should be advised. However, most guilt is not as serious as that experienced in combat situations or natural disasters.

Guilt for many people is similar to generalized anxiety disorder. It is there like a cloud over one's head and the key point to remember is that you cannot change the past. When I inquire about this guilt, many people have to think for a while to get a handle on it. A typical response is, "If I had only given my son more support he would have some direction in his life." Another example is, "If I had taken the time to visit her while she was healthy, we would have had a better relationship."

We often do not make the best choices and we would have done some things differently if given the opportunity. In some cases, it is appropriate to make amends to another. This has been a component in 12-step programs for many years. In other cases, we just need to move on.

The baggage of guilt can be based on thoughts rather than on actions. There are some who feel guilty about their thoughts. This is usually a sign of some punitive, guilt-ridden past and some will frame these thoughts as impure. We all have impure thoughts. It is when thoughts are converted to action that they can cause us problems. Some of the process of leaving guilt behind is abandoning those beliefs that we should be as pure as a deity and we should feel guilty when we do not measure up to this expectation.

Remember that we can learn to quiet our minds and actually experience a total lack of thought. It is when we can quiet our minds that we can listen. Regardless of a person's belief in the spiritual aspects of life, knowing that there is benefit to quieting the mind allows us to clean our minds of wasted thoughts that distort our reality and cause us pain and suffering.

Use an everyday symbol in your life to keep you on track with discarding mental garbage. Every time that you throw out a trash bag, think of this as a metaphor of discarding unproductive thoughts. You may find it helpful to first prioritize those thoughts that really need to go. For example this week decide to toss your wasteful opinions about others that don't really serve a purpose.

I truly believe that much of the content of our thinking is similar to pollution in a stream. Our mental ecology is polluted by resentment, criticism, guilt, and fear. The water becomes murky, stagnant and the flow slows. Keep this analogy in mind as we enter our discussion on our economy of personal energy in the next chapter.

Our Economy
of Energy

Our use of energy can sabotage our ability to change and to maintain change. If you have some frame-of-reference for cell biology, chemistry, physics or other science, you know that everything in the universes is comprised of energy. However, we will not delve into discussions on quantum holograms, discontinuities or other physical linkages. The only point that is a key to energy and to science is that everything in the universe is connected by energy.

There are many great analogies to use when discussing energy and the problems caused when there is too little energy or when energy is misdirected. If you have a garden hose that has holes in it throughout the length of the hose, the water pressure is diminished at the end. As you patch the leaks, the water pressure increases. A small hole in the middle of your vacuum cleaner hose can diminish the suction. There are many factors that can rob and thus diminish your personal energy.

Energy can be spent like currency, therefore I will use terms that typically relate to economics in my discussion of energy. Energy and time are related in that during any given period of time we can expend various amounts of energy. Except for the most enlightened among us, both energy and time are limited commodities. However, we usually underestimate how much of both we really have.

Our personal energy is divided into our mental and physical energy. For the sake of simplicity, we will place emotional and spiritual energy under the heading of mental energy. Because we mentally call upon our physical energy, we cannot really separate our forms of personal energy. With the exception of the autonomic nervous system, our thoughts directly control our actions. Thus the focus here will be on the expenditure of our mental energy, much in same way that chapter two focused on the use of mental time.

In the previous two chapters, I mentioned that obsessing about why others think and behave as they do uses valuable time and is garbage that needs to be purged from your mind. This issue falls into that category of things that you cannot change. A different way of looking at these types of problems is that you don't need to finance any myths about the control that one person or group has over another. If someone in the public eye has done something to bring a firestorm of criticism down on himself, you don't need to finance this with your energy. This is a poor investment and is similar to investing in stock that is on the way down with little chance of increasing in value.

If people who constantly gossip about others surround you, you don't need to finance this activity with your energy. When in the midst of those who are fearful about things that they have no control over, you don't need to finance their fear with your energy.

These sorts of activities take your energy and your time. If people didn't finance activities that lead to hate, prejudice and egocentric thinking, these activities would dry up and blow away. Although we know that there will always be those who feed on such things and who always find others to perpetuate these activities, we can withdraw our investment in fueling these fires.

The difficulty comes when you don't know how to spend your mental energy wisely. If you don't know what you really enjoy and don't have priorities, it is easy to invest your mental energy in anything that comes along. Lack of direction makes it easy to tie up your energy in gossip, tabloid news and other people's shortcomings. This is analogous to what some of the working poor do: spend all of their money on payday because they cannot imagine living on a budget or thinking about any real financial security.

For those who do not know how to best spend their mental energy, it is very easy to have an energy blockage. If you find yourself angry, resentful, judgmental or emotionally upset for any extended period of time, your mental energy becomes blocked. This process is analogous to the arteries of the heart becoming blocked. Our energy cannot flow when it is blocked by our emotions and ruminating thoughts.

When we want to communicate something important and cannot, our energy becomes blocked. Whether this is due to our own inability to communicate our feelings or to someone else who doesn't know how to listen and respond, the results are the same.

Energy becomes blocked when we have incomplete projects in our lives. We must either complete those things that we have started or reevaluate them and deem them less significant. Incomplete projects or initiatives and indecision stop us in our tracks and stop our flow of energy. When we don't do what we say we are going to do, others don't take us seriously and we begin to question our own ability to complete tasks. We stop taking our ability to complete projects seriously and thus lower our expectations of ourselves.

In addition to energy blockages, there are energy leaks. This problem is exhibited by those who possess a lot of energy, but who don't know how to focus this energy toward a rewarding outcome. Seeing such a person is like watching an octopus on rollerblades. They are all over the place and find it difficult to complete anything.

When I am lecturing on the topic of peak performance, I can always tap into people's frame of reference for being in the high-energy zone. We have all had those days when we get out of bed and feel as if we can do anything. We clean that garage or basement that has been growing into a nightmare of clutter and disorganization. We may paint a few rooms or rearrange our closets. Everyone seems to have a frame of reference for this high-energy feeling. Here we see the direct relationship between our mental and physical energy. Our attitudes are good, we are focused, and our bodies respond with the physical energy to get the job done.

The secret is to know how to replicate this feeling with increased frequency. Maintaining many of our life changes requires enthusiasm and high energy. Having access to high energy is extremely self-reinforcing. Knowing that we must maintain change on our low energy days will lead us to doing all of those things that give us a positive and uplifting attitude. Without the emotional component of feeling responsive to the outcomes of change, our energy drops and we quit. Simply thinking about why we should complete a task frequently isn't enough.

As soon as you get out of bed, go into the bathroom and look into the mirror and say to yourself, "I determine my attitude for today! I choose to look at today with enthusiasm and with optimism! Others don't control how I feel!" Positive affirmations are not tricks; they are honest statements that remind you of what and who you have control over. You have control over you and a part of this is your attitude and how you invest your energy.

Some people seem to have an inordinate concern about their own energy conservation. Perhaps they believe that if they do not expend much energy during their early and middle years, they will have more to spend when they retire. Others seem to believe that if they expend too much of their energy at the beginning of the week, they will not have enough energy to enjoy their weekend. Neither physical nor mental energy works this way: we create energy by using energy. If we receive adequate exercise, sleep and nutrition, we don't need to worry about storing energy.

There are many sayings that refer to this process and some of the most common are as follows:

- We get back what we put in.
- We attract to us what we are.
- How can we expect to get something different when we continue to do the same things?
- Laughter is infectious.
- Let go and let God.

Each of these statements addresses our economy of energy— the ways we spend our energy. If you cannot connect these statements to energy, stop and spend some time trying to make these connections.

There are some differences between our financial and our energy economy. If we make $7000 each month, this is what we have to work with—we can budget for basic needs, savings, entertainment, gifts, etc. Our energy economy is very different. Our energy economy is more like getting rebates and a percent back on the amount that we spend. In our energy economy we can go into a store, purchase a few items, and come out with more in our wallet than we had when we entered. We can invest a little on a regular basis and receive 1000 percent interest within a year or two. Your energy economy is much more interesting than your financial economy—even if you are a millionaire.

For the sake of this discussion, let us assume that we have energy units. There are physical and mental energy units and neither are mutually exclusive of the other. Let us assume that we begin each day with 100 units of each. We eat breakfast and go to work. During this process we think about our plans for our workday and about the things that we accomplished yesterday. During our morning at work we get into a conversation about yesterday's game and whether a romance between two celebrities is on or off. We wonder whether we should have told a co-worker about something personal last Friday and whether we should have attended the optional training for a new computer program. Before lunch we have thought about four possible poor decisions and many scenarios that range from not getting promoted to being talked about behind our back.

If this scenario sounds like a wasteful and energy-burning mess, you are correct: it's a scenario about nothing. We spend much of our mental and physical energy with inane thoughts and actions. Why do we do this? We like to keep our plates full and we like to feel significant. If we can't keep our plate filled with good stuff, we fill it with crap. If we aren't really important, we make ourselves the center of the universe and it is all about us. Yesterday's game, a movie star's relationship, and what you told someone last week is all like cheap filler in a bad meatloaf.

Most people do not obsess about you. They have their own lives to live, their own set of problems, and their own agendas for life. You are not typically included in their agenda. They do not really care what you think. In short, it is not really all about you so don't waste your time and energy feeding your ego.

I have worked with clients in therapy who love to say, "I do not like that." "That" refers to the family members being out late at night or going to a part of town that they do not believe to be safe. They spend a lot of time and energy not liking people, places, things and events. In reality no one really cares what he or she likes or does not like. It's just wasted time and energy.

The more self-centered you are, the more self-centered fear you will possess. Self-centeredness can be defined as how much you believe that the world revolves around you. If you believe that your needs are much greater and/or more important than those of others, self-centered fear may be at the root of this thinking. The fear emanates from fear of how important you really are in context to others. Fear of not being important or special drives the ego to assure that you don't feel less than what you believe that you should be.

Self-centered fear is the master energy thief of all time. Look at what you really fear and make a list. For those who wish to get a handle on making and maintaining personal change, this is a great place to begin. Fear leads to insecurity, lack of competence, a feeling of being out of control and a questioning of everything. Fear is the antithesis of love, serenity and the feeling of wellbeing. Make a list of your fears before you begin any change process.

In your personal energy economy you have choices about how you expend your physical and mental energy. As previously stated, the number one reason people say they do not exercise is time restraint. Nonetheless these same people will waste much of their time. How we spend our energy and time is a matter of setting priorities. How important is exercise in your life? If it is not important, you are not likely to do it. If it is important, you will make the time. Some people exercise while they watch TV or movies, some people exercise early before going to work, and others exercise during lunchtime. What people receive in return is more energy, better health and a clearer mind. These are the types of rewards that people consider when they are doing their cost/benefit analysis—the focus of the next chapter.

Make a list of those things that you know that you should do and yet don't do. This list usually includes things such as making better food choices, exercising, being less critical and being kind to those people whom you don't like. Next, make a list of those things that you shouldn't do, but do anyway. Examples of these things include gossip, reading inane material, watching too much TV, eating under stress, and trying to control other people and ruminating about things that you cannot change. As you look at these two lists, be aware of the mental energy involved in both lists. One revelation that may occur is that you can simply unplug from items on list two and plug that energy savings into list one.

The biggest sabotage to switching from one list to the other is feelings of guilt. If you are constantly feeling guilty for pigging out, not exercising, being unfriendly or other behavior that you really don't like in yourself, you are stuck in tearing down your own self-worth. Move out of guilt to acceptance of yourself so that you don't continue self-deprecating feelings about yourself. How can you love others unless you love yourself? How can you accomplish change if you don't feel worthy of change?

You can change personal agendas that have you stuck and that can rob you of energy that could be used for other things. We all know those who seem to bear a burden of personal agendas that neither have purpose nor meaning.

Because I am a frequent flyer, I overhear a lot of conversations between strangers. When I sit near the same people on multiple flights, I often hear their personal agendas. On a recent flight I overheard a middle-age guy work his agenda into conversations with two passengers on two consecutive flights. His agenda was that we should tell it like it is when discussing HIV/AIDS. This was based on how gay males, in west coast bathhouses, were having sex with multiple partners and how this had caused the entire AIDS epidemic. I was sat near this one person for about five hours and could imagine how much energy he expended on this item. Inaccuracies aside, he was stuck in this agenda and it was robbing him of energy, time and serenity.

Self-centered fear is usually very apparent. Whether this man feared being gay, hated gays, or wanted to somehow relate that he was concerned about the world becoming gay and everyone dying of AIDS, he was clearly fearful. He was similar to a person who stays focused on those he hates because he is afraid to look at his own life. This is an excellent example of self-centered fear.

Give some thought to your agenda items and reality test the importance of wasted time and energy to convince others or yourself that you are right. If suddenly everyone agreed with the person with a strong agenda item, what would happen? Do you think that they would drop their need to be right? No, they would simply find another agenda item. It is not about winning or losing, it is about feeling superior or one-up. They know the real truth and others do not.

You can use your energy to further the happiness and serenity of yourself and others or you can constantly use your energy to fight battles to no great end. The energy that comes with serenity is incredibly powerful and allows one to focus on improving lives. Those on this path have small egos and influence others to take a similar path by serving as models.

One laudable goal may be to learn to maintain change and continually improve while using low energy. If you work toward harmony with all that exists you will thrive with change and growth. Energy isn't a factor that more is always better. The energy from a laser is focused and can perform significant tasks. Realize that having more energy is an excellent starting place. Once you have more energy, work toward focus and deriving energy from a willingness to accept yourself as a divine being capable of love, joy and peace.

There is a great deal to be learned from "energy work." How we use and store different types of energy can be useful when pursuing change. Yogi, meditation, prayer, and other methods of evaluating one's energy can open many pathways to personal growth.

5 Cost/Benefit Analysis

When we observe people who continue to fail at making and maintaining a change, we sometimes believe they are not trying hard enough or that they just do not want the change badly enough. After working with those who struggle with making and maintaining change, I have noted that many fail due to the unrecognized dynamics of the cost/benefit analysis.

Some of the most-fit middle-aged men once had well-defined washboard abs. With age, a layer of body fat covers the abdominal muscles. If the person continues the exercises that originally developed these well-defined muscles, they will still be there. However, the layer of body fat covers these muscles as body weight shifts during the aging process.

During my 50s, I decided that I wanted to reverse the trend toward increased body fat in my mid-section and regain my washboard abs. I cut my consumption of fats, sugar, and carbohydrates and increased my protein intake. Also, I increased my regimen of abdominal exercises. After six months, I had made some notable progress.

After completing a cost/benefit analysis of my goal, I dropped this goal. I had determined that I was not willing to pay the price of time, effort, and dietary changes to pursue this goal. I did not say that I could not achieve this goal; I said that I was not willing to pay the cost. I did not see the benefit was worth the cost. Stop and think for a minute about how many times you have intentionally said that achieving a goal was not worth the cost?

This very simple and personal example shows how an internal cost/benefit analysis is key to our change efforts. If we cannot be honest with ourselves, we will likely sabotage our change efforts. Assuming that we will naturally pay the cost of change is unrealistic.

When lecturing on the topics of maintaining change and continuous quality improvement, I frequently observe looks of disbelief and confusion from my audience when I mention cost/benefit analysis. Most people equate this term with economics. However, we all use this process without using this particular title. I use examples that apply to my social work students.

When social workers remove children from a home due to some form of child maltreatment, the custodial parent or parents perform a cost/benefit analysis at some point. The social worker will typically, in conjunction with the client and significant others, work out a case plan that would lead to the reunification of the child or children with the parent(s). This plan may mandate parent training, substance abuse treatment and monitoring, anger management classes and an array of other stipulations.

Custodial parents are left with making a decision about whether they are willing to pay the cost in time, effort and sometimes money to have their children reunited with them. Some young and inexperienced social workers believe that this is a simple issue and say, "Of course they want their children back at any cost." But no, some parents decide that the time and energy required to make the stipulated changes are not worth it. A few parents will say this up front, but most will simply sabotage the case planning so that reunification does not occur.

The dynamics of the cost/benefit analysis are constantly being weighed by each of us, but these dynamics often occur under our radar. Always intentionally ask yourself whether the benefit of the change that you are contemplating is worth the cost. Some people never do this and find they constantly trying to achieve a goal without every knowing why they do not succeed.

Before reading further, be aware that some of the following examples may test your knowledge of points that I have discussed thus far. Keep in mind that when others complete their own cost/benefit analysis they may arrive at a completely different decision than you. However, this is their decision. If you spend a lot of time and energy thinking about their decision and how it is wrong, go back and reread the last four chapters until the lessons become crystal clear.

Our change efforts often are not permanent because we don't complete a cost/benefit analysis. We get started on making a change and we fall off the change train and don't really know what happened. To accomplish a sense of personal clarity think about the benefits versus cost of a change and then discuss this with another person.

When you decide that making a change is not worth the cost—as I related in my example about washboard abs—consider if you are being honest with yourself. When you are insincere with yourself, you know it. Guilt and shame then underlies your motivation to make any change. As stated in the last chapter, you have then stepped into the sabotage of low self-worth and low energy.

Unless you are conscious of your cost/benefit analysis, you may never know what is happening when you fail to make and maintain your target change. When considering a change, put your thoughts and feelings about the costs versus the benefit up-front and under great personal scrutiny. Realize the importance of trusting yourself with accurately assessing your self-honesty.

Advertising media continuously tells us how we should act, look and think. This ongoing exposure does not allow us to say honestly to ourselves that we do not wish to fit a particular image or participate in a newly accepted trend. What kind of person would think this way? Thus, we have plenty of assistance with not being honest with ourselves.

I have lost friends and family members due to diabetes. They all knew what they needed to do to keep the disease under control, but they each made their own choices. Some were still eating the worst possible foods even after limbs had been amputated and sight was gone. I imagine that we all know people who have died from lung cancer. I know young women with three to five children, graduate degrees, and plenty of money that continue to smoke. They continue because they fear gaining weight if they stop smoking (and they may). Their cost/benefit analysis has led them to a decision to continue smoking. When I look at others, I frame the results of cost/benefit analysis as neither good nor bad; they simply are. People simply don't have a common set of priorities.

One of the major variables in performing a cost/benefit analysis is discomfort. Our level of discomfort is often the impetus behind change. People get out of bad relationships, make geographic moves, return to school and change careers out of discomfort. However, everyone has a different measure of discomfort and of hitting bottom. Some of us have a very high bottom and little tolerance for discomfort while others have a high tolerance for discomfort and a very low bottom. It is worth determining where your tolerance level for discomfort lies. How bad does something have to get before you are ready to make a commitment to change?

In today's economy, people slowly find that their tolerance for discomfort gradually increases. I know of people who are beginning their second year of unemployment and they have adjusted to having much less. Thus discomfort for them may not be the motivator that will be life changing. This is neither good nor bad; it involves a re-evaluation of what is important and what is intolerable.

How long does it take before you forget how bad things once were? This is a problem for many people. Our memories seem to be short when it comes to remembering pain and suffering. Some of this is denial that things were ever that bad and some of it is selective memory. It is always useful to keep difficult times in your memory so that these thoughts and accompanying feelings can be readily accessible. As you will see in the second half of *Stop the Sabotage*, we need to have access to both our weaknesses and our strengths when working on making and maintaining change.

A thorough cost/benefit analysis should be done periodically for those changes that you simply have not been able to maintain. The costs and benefits for the same desired change is forever changing. The price of some changes may become less once children start school or leave for college. Our maturational process sometimes allows us to shed baggage, as we can become more independent, care less about what others think and/or improve our social networks.

One major variable in completing a well-thought out cost/benefit analysis is one's ability to delay gratification. Some changes take a major commitment of time, energy and money. For a working adult to acquire a degree, they must make sacrifices and have faith that their investment will pay dividends. It is often best to reframe the dividends. For example, rather than ask the question whether you will make more money with a degree or an additional degree, ask to what extent you will improve your current quality of life? For those who place more emphasis on achieving their life's destiny ask how additional credentials can contribute to life's objectives and to the wellbeing of others.

The completion of a cost/benefit analysis should be a beginning step in planning your strategy for change. If you cannot clearly see that the benefit is worth the cost, select something that is easier or select a segment of the change that you wish to address. One way to look at segmenting a change is to look at the entire process and determine what parts you can most readily accomplish.

Revisit the process of cost/benefit analysis as you read chapter 9 on the topic of visualizing how you will look, act and feel differently once you have made this change. Find someone who has accomplished the change that you wish to make. Inquire about their process and how they managed to accomplish the change. Once you have done all that you can do to obtain a clear picture of the benefits of the change process, reevaluate the cost versus the benefit.

Without this simple step of completing a cost/benefit analysis, many well-meaning people are stopped from initiating and/or completing a change. One of the reasons this step is seldom mentioned in self-help books is because writers tend to tread lightly on the topic of personal honesty.

The authors of books found in the "Recovery" section of a bookstore typically discuss and promote self-honesty. The difference between people who are generally reading self-help material and those who are reading recovery material is that those in recovery will often die unless they make and maintain serious changes in their life. There is much to be gained from reading recovery-based literature.

If you determine that you cannot discern real benefit from change, you are faced with the choice of stopping your process or with moving forward regardless. Many of us will move forward because we know that the change is beneficial, but we cannot feel a sense of knowing that the change will be rewarding enough to proceed. This process is sometimes referred to "acting in faith" or "acting as if"—you have made your desired change and you can feel the benefit. If you determine that this will be your path, you certainly can succeed.

Change can be self-gratifying if you allow yourself to feel the rewards. People who are working on health-related changes may find that they can climb a flight of stairs that they once could not climb. They can play with a child or grandchild with whom they have never been able to play. Those working on attitudinal changes may find that the general public is much more friendly and cooperative or that life is not nearly as gloomy as they once thought.

These little benefits, while not earth shattering, can be rewarding enough to motivate and inspire. When these small benefits occur and are felt, a person can reevaluate the cost/benefit and find more benefit than cost. Many times the beginning steps of a change are the most difficult.

Staying up to date with yourself and monitoring where you are in relation to your cost/benefit analysis is key to success. Remember that self-honesty will keep you current with yourself and your goals.

Clarity of the Issues

Now that we have discussed many of the primary sabotages of maintaining change, you are ready to move forward. The first section of *Stop the Sabotage* (chapters 1-5) has set the stage for change by addressing some of the most common difficulties that people experience when undertaking the change process.

For many years I have used a simple contract for assisting others in making change. I have used these steps and have found that they work well for me and for those I serve. Currently, I use these steps in a six-hour continuing education course on the topic of Continuous Quality Improvement (CQI).

The steps are as follows:

1. What I want to change is...

2. The amount of time that it will take to make this change is...

3. The type of support that I need to make this change is...

4. How I will look, act, and feel differently after I make this change is…

5. How I might sabotage this change is…

6. How I will utilize my frame of reference for successful change is…

This chapter will assist you in making some additional determinations regarding step one of this contract. My observation about people who struggle with change is that they often have their plan for change in the wrong order or they are not sure where to begin. Everything has a natural order, but people seem to jump into the change process at all points.

There is an abundance of information about making changes. There is much less information on determining where to begin and how to maintain change once the person has begun the change process.

In the first step of problem identification, we must determine whether the change that we wish to make is based on a primary problem or a symptom of a problem. Although both are problems and can be equally uncomfortable on a daily basis, there is a difference. Treating a symptom will give you symptom relief, but the problem will remain. As an example, let us compare the medical model for treating disease.

There is not a cure for some medical problems; we can only treat the symptoms. Herpes cannot be cured, but it can be controlled by medication. An alcoholic cannot be cured, but a daily reprieve from drinking is certainly possible. Some forms of cancer, if caught early enough, can be treated and cured.

There isn't anything wrong about pursuing symptom relief instead of a cure. However, it is helpful to know the difference as it relates to the change that you plan to pursue. Symptom relief may require more maintenance and ongoing work. This can be a real positive for the remainder of your life. If your change culminates in a lifestyle change, you and those who love and care for you will benefit. People who have a genetic predisposition toward obesity can lose the weight and can keep the weight off. However, this involves permanent lifestyle changes. These changes are healthy and will benefit the person throughout his or her life.

Students have often asked me to explain the difference between counseling and psychotherapy. In explaining the difference, I often address some of the ways to differentiate between first order change and symptom relief. Psychotherapy takes an historical approach, addressing issues that cause people to make the life decisions that they make. It looks at your history. Psychotherapy involves reworking old decisions that no longer work and realizing how you got to where you are. It involves going back and fixing things at their root cause, changing your programming.

Counseling, on the other hand, is more focused in the here and now. It can bring about revelations and epiphanies based on past decisions. The counseling process assists in reality testing, gaining new skills, and in allowing one to clearly articulate thoughts and feelings to a non-judgmental person. Regarding programming, you may become aware that much of what you believe is nothing more than social programming. This realization can go a long way toward not buying into beliefs that aren't based in reality.

We know that some people who learn more about their particular physical or psychiatric diagnosis can begin exhibiting more of the symptoms. Others will determine that they have a genetic predisposition for a condition and then feel helpless and hopeless. They then think themselves into illness, obesity, and neurotic behavior. They operate out of the very low energy positions of shame, guilt and apathy. Our thoughts play a major role in outcome.

When symptom relief becomes part of your life, I argue that you may very often deal with old issues. I see this in people who I had thought 20 years ago were destined to suffer from personality disorders. Through group affiliation and the methodology used in 12-step programs, they are now very whole and happy individuals with long-term relationships and productive lives that include giving back to the general welfare of society. In working a lifelong program, people develop long-term consistency in using tried and true principles and steps on a daily basis, while having a large support network of those who have knowledge of their issues. This process is self-reinforcing and leads to one's efforts to maintain change.

Although the contract noted above can be extremely useful, it may require some rearranging to assure maximum success. I have dedicated a chapter to each of the six steps in the change contract. Take a close look at the steps. You may decide that you want to first determine the answer to step 5 (sabotages)—especially if you have attempted your target change and have failed. Although the first five chapters and chapter 10 discuss sabotages, there are many more. It is important to understand what has stopped you in the past before moving forward.

If you have completed a cost-benefit analysis and have determined that the reason that you have failed is because the benefit is marginal (given the cost), you may want to begin with step four (how you will look and feel differently after you complete your change). Determine where you should begin based on your knowledge of yourself. If you need feedback due to internal confusion, go to step three and reach out for feedback from others, rather than listening to that committee in your head that can sometimes tie you into an inconclusive knot for long periods of time.

Why do you want to make a change? A common reason for making change is discomfort or a need to improve one's life. As I stated in the last chapter, discomfort is the primary motivator for change. Discomfort is a fascinating dynamic because people have varying levels of what they will tolerate. For those who must hit their bottom before deciding to make and maintain a change, the bottom can be difficult to reach. One well-meaning friend, family member, employer, or other entity can stop a person from reaching that all-important bottom. One's level of discomfort is relative to many variables. Let us explore some examples of the relative nature of discomfort.

When we identify a problem for possible change, we often consider the seriousness of the problem and how others would see the seriousness of this problem. If the problem is serious to us, but we do not believe that it will be considered a big deal to others, we often do not pursue the support that we need for change. The importance of a problem is relative to a person's life experiences and coping skills. You are the expert on your feelings and identifying the areas that you wish to change.

If your target change is to increase assertiveness at work, those within your personal life may not see the need for this change. Friends may not know that you work with a group of highly assertive co-workers, supervisors and managers. Those in one part of our life may not have a frame-of-reference for the realities in other parts of our life. We best know what we need to personally accomplish to be happy.

Many years ago I was teaching an introductory psychology class at a local community college. One evening a young lady appeared in the hall after I had begun my lecture. I could see that she had cried to the point of hyperventilating. I excused myself from my class and went into the hall to see if I could determine the problem and to offer assistance. When she could finally talk, she related the story of her current discomfort.

As a high school graduation gift, her parents had given her a new 5-Series BMW. They had gone to Europe for three weeks and she was left home alone. When it was time to leave for class, she could not open the garage door. She said that she pushed the wall-mounted buttons and the ones on her remote and nothing worked. She finally went next door to seek assistance and a neighbor opened the door for her. This made her 20 minutes late for class. This inability to open the garage door was the reason for her high level of distress.

Although it is often easy to discount the distress of others by comparing those things that would distress us, this does not change the fact that distress and discomfort is relative to many factors. Everyone has a different tolerance of stress and our definition of stress is dependent of many variables. Think about times when you discounted someone's distress level when you did not think it rose to your definition for distress and discomfort.

There are important lessons to be learned from looking at how we compare ourselves to others. Earlier I mentioned that our ego likes to constantly play the game of determining whether people are either like us or not like us. As a result, we often determine that we are either better than or worse than others. One reason that we compare ourselves to others is to blemish another person, idea, place, or thing and to make ourselves special or better than others. Instead of wasting time and energy on better than or less than thinking, look at your needs and the best approaches to make and maintain your change.

When we need support on an issue that we think others will discount, we will often begin to discount the issue's importance. However, this change may be the one that will take us where we wish to be. For example, your ability to focus on one task at a time may be seen as trivial by some, but this may be the primary issue that is sabotaging your effort to make and to maintain change.

If you believe that maintaining a change is related to old survival decisions, you may want to seek professional help. For example, if you have been a victim of any type of sexual abuse, you may decide to utilize a mental health professional to discuss your survival decisions. One common issue among this population is being overweight because eating has served as a survival mechanism. This sort of issue can remain buried and out of one's awareness.

When someone is struggling to change something in his or her life because life isn't working, take a look at a few basics. We are what we think about. If our thoughts are negative, critical, and deficit focused this is what we will manifest. Using this simple fact, one place to begin a change contract would be to think about who you wish to become instead of things you wish to have. Work from a "to be" list instead of a "to have" list.

If you feel as if you want to make changes in your life, but cannot put your finger on exactly where to start there are a few basics to ponder. The goal of making a change to be a more loving, caring and intentional person addresses many significant issues. This change decreases the ego's hold on you and your beliefs that you are a separate being instead of being part of something much larger than yourself. Whether you consider this to be an altruistic, heuristic, spiritual or utilitarian move toward self-improvement, it would put you further along on the path to love, peace and self-actualization.

Changes in attitude often follow changes in behavior. If you change your behavior, your attitude will often follow. I have seen many concrete examples of this process. For example, research has shown that a parent's level of support for a child that is self-identified as LGBTQ (lesbian, gay, bi-sexual, transgender, or questioning) greatly impacts a number of outcomes in the child's life while reducing risk factors. After parents have shown supportive behavior for a period of time, their attitudes often align with their behavior.

The alignment of attitude and behavior is a two-way street. Whatever changes first, the other is likely to follow. For example you can determine whether you decide to join a conversation where friends or co-workers are negatively gossiping about someone you hardy know. In these situations, any passive agreement with the conversation puts you in a place of justifying your agreement. Now you are on the path toward not liking someone that you really don't know.

When we cross over a line of committing ourselves by stating a verbal agreement with a group, we are faced with a decision. The decision is to either justify these actions or to tell ourselves that we made a poor decision. Guess which choice we usually make? We do this with individuals and with groups.

If the change that you are working toward is focused on growing your network of real friends and to respect the opinion of others, you may wish to cease jumping on-board the gossip bandwagon.

The next five chapters cover steps two through six of the change contract presented at the beginning of this chapter. I suggest placing this contract on your computer or in a notebook where you can actually sign it. This small step can make it real and help you to own your change. Also this small step allows you to personalize this information in a way different from reading a novel, where the book is about others. *Stop the Sabotage* is about you in a very personal way.

A Plan and Timeline for Change

Many of us have heard the saying, "if we fail to plan, we plan to fail." Planning is important, but we can also simply get out of bed one morning and decide to go to the beach or mountains for a few days. The entire experience can be wonderful and can go without a hitch. However, our expectations for this type of trip aren't to make a life change. Our plans are to relax and enjoy our experience. This experience will have a beginning, middle and end.

However, some changes are like this last minute decision to take a vacation. They have completion dates while other changes go on for the remainder of life. Regardless of whether the change is long or short-term, a schedule includes the component steps for the change. When deciding on the steps to achieve change, we can take the opportunity to more closely examine the change that we wish to make. During this process we can determine how to prioritize the steps and we can usually discern which steps will be the most difficult.

When people have a goal of losing weight, they need to continue with the changes that cause them to lose the weight. We know that diets seldom work and that lifestyle changes keep the weight off. Some people say that they want to stop drinking and they are not alcoholic; they can stop or alter their alcohol intake. However, the alcoholic cannot stop for a while and then drink normally. Thus it is important to know which changes will take ongoing maintenance and which ones have an endpoint.

Creating a plan and an accompanying timeline for achieving the plan will prevent procrastination, a well-known sabotage. One of the stages of making a change is information gathering. In this stage, we research the information needed to assure us that we know all we need to know to make our change. In many ways, *Stop the Sabotage* fulfills this need for making and maintaining some changes. However, people get stuck at the information gathering stage; they always want to read one more article or talk to one more person. I have known people to get stuck at this stage for years.

There are a number of reasons why this occurs. One is magical thinking. People believe that there must be one magic bullet out there that will make their change easy; all they must do is to keep looking. Others stay stuck at the information gathering stage because they are fearful of getting started. Saying that you are still researching the issues sounds good but in actual fact nothing is happening. When you set a timeline, define your steps and get started. You are then on your way to accomplishing your goals.

Because I have two national certifications as a personal trainer and write about fitness and wellness, people frequently ask me about exercise gadgets that they see on infomercials. Most of them have some value. However they are often surprised when they realize that using the gadget isn't enough; they must actually perform supplemental cardiovascular exercise and/or follow nutritional guidelines. The magic bullet to fitness is extremely rare.

An inherent part of determining a timeline for change is working on a reasonable plan that includes short-term goals. There are many ways of looking at setting short-term goals. You may be aware of the process of successive approximation. This process is often used to conquer fears that could be categorized as phobias. For example, if you have a fear of flying to the point that you will not fly, you can attend classes to overcome this fear. After completing your internal cost/benefit analysis to determine whether the benefits of flying would outweigh the cost, you would proceed. Perhaps you are interviewing for a job that requires monthly flights across the country and you really want this particular job.

The successive approximation process takes you through a number of baby steps. First you may only go to the airport. Then a future step may be to board a private plane but not take off. Some organizations may offer an opportunity to sit in a flight simulator. During this process, people are slowly desensitized from the fear of flying. The final step is to actually board a plane, take off, and land. People who go through this experience can process their feelings and work through their fears.

Although most readers of *Stop the Sabotage* are not looking to conquer phobic behavior, please realize that this type of process is applicable to many types of change. If a behavioral goal is to develop social skills so you feel comfortable in groups and can meet interesting people, you may not want to start by mixing at a large political fund raising event. If your socialization skills are limited to small talk at work and brief bar conversations after work, you may want to begin your change with joining a group that shares a common interest, a civic organization or a Toastmasters' club.

Realize that you want to slowly build your confidence, not set yourself up for immediate failure.

Planning does not mean putting all of your eggs in one basket. In the example above, you could simultaneously learn a new vocabulary word each day and listen to an hour of public radio or watch PBS for news instead of sensationalized tabloid news. Subscribing to interesting podcasts offers fresh ideas. Your planning should have a multifaceted approach.

When embarking on a change process, always ask yourself, "How will I maintain my change?" If we stop doing something or we begin a new behavior, what length of success do we personally need before we are comfortable with our change? When will your change not require as much expenditure of energy to keep the change going? For changes that include accomplishments such as finding a job, completing a degree or finding a partner we can set a schedule.

Part of setting a realistic schedule involves the mechanics of accomplishing component parts. If your goal is to change jobs, you can set a time to complete your resume. You can set a time frame for posting your resume on four national Internet employment sites. Once your resume' has been received by a potential employer, you can follow up on a regular schedule. You can set a minimum number of resumes that you will send out per week and track the responses and follow-up emails and calls. You can set a time limit on using a particular methodology and have another method of attack if your current method doesn't produce results. However, you can use different methods concurrently. For example, you could simultaneously search Internet sites, newspapers and professional publications in addition to attending job fairs and utilizing employment services.

If the change that we are striving for has a beginning, middle and end, some attention should be paid to how you will continue the change once you feel you have reached your goal. When will you be coasting? There is an old saying that nothing can coast on level ground. Give this some thought. If you are coasting, what are you really doing? With this answer in mind, what can you build into your change process to assure that you don't begin coasting?

There is much to be learned from the methodology of 12-step programs. If we have a problem with obsessive thinking and/or compulsive behaviors, we can look at small increments of time. Many people set a goal of being more optimistic and less negative. If one has a long-term pattern of such problems, an entire week of thinking more positively can seem like an eternity. When you can say to yourself that you are not going to be negative today, right now, you have a day under your belt. Before you know it, you have a week and then a month of success.

Perhaps a more productive method of addressing this issue of being negative is to not focus on what you are not going to be. Focus on being positive in your thinking and actions. Go out of your way to be friendly and to meet inspirational and motivational people. Focus on gratitude instead of those things that you don't have.

When I volunteer at a local homeless shelter, I meet inspirational and motivational people that have a positive impact on me. Some of the residents inspire and motivate me more than any motivational speaker I may have paid to hear. Remember my message from chapter one—you can learn important lessons from anyone in any place at any time.

With the current economic climate in America, a growing number of people are working on changing their feelings of prejudice and their behavior of discrimination. People are listening to themselves and not liking what they hear. Those who have lost jobs are finding themselves in the shoes of those they once frowned upon.

This process of improving our attitudes about others is a one-day-at–a-time process that quickly reinforces itself. When the negative feelings of fear-based emotions such as hatred and intolerance are converted to compassion, love and understanding we have more energy, time, inspiration and motivation to continue our change. It feels rewarding when the list of people like you becomes longer and the list of people not like you become shorter. At the end of the day, people have much more in common than they have differences.

The dynamics of the self-reinforcing aspects of change goes back to the end of chapter five (Cost/Benefit Analysis) when we discussed going ahead with pursuing your change process when the benefit is not totally clear. Sometimes self-reinforcing behavior is not necessarily the good feelings that we receive for doing something better or different. It is reinforcing because we don't feel the discomfort that we have felt for so long. For example, if you are one of those people who are always tired and you have decided that you are tired of being tired, it is self-reinforcing when you aren't feeling that way. If your change has focused on health related changes (e.g., exercise or better food choices) or on being less self-centered, you will probably not feel so tired. The self-reinforcement may come from not feeling awful rather than initially feeling wonderful.

Make a thorough plan for making your change that includes short-term goals with accompanying time frames. Consider those things that have and have not worked in the past. Allow yourself to see all of the possibilities that this change will entail. Now you are ready to develop and use your support network that we are about to discuss.

There are infinite possibilities for outcomes when you embrace change. Some of these possibilities may far surpass your initial goals. As you open yourself up for change, keep doing the next right thing. If you take a step backwards, don't throw in the towel and begin running off the low energy emotions of guilt and shame.

Developing and Utilizing Support

8

The second part of the change contract entails determining the type of support needed to assure that your change will occur. Support is extremely important. How many times have you made a secret New Year's resolution and broken it within the first week of the New Year? Simply by telling others about your intended change can go a long ways towards ensuring that you will stick to your plan.

My observation about support is that this process keeps you out of your head. Unless we interact with others before and during our change process, we are likely to stay in our head and in our own ego. Our ego is full of such defenses as justifications, intellectualizations, rationalizations, projections, denial and all sorts of other counter-productive means of sabotaging ourselves. Without support we get into our own loop of obsessive thinking. Little thoughts quickly grow out of proportion and become abstract, taking on a life of their own.

In today's electronic age, it is easy to have one-way communication and think that it is support. I can BLOG or PODCAST my need for assistance about any area where I am seeking change, but the results aren't the same as speaking eye-to-eye with an individual of my own choosing. One-way communication or random communications with strangers may be interesting, but this can take one far from the intended and intentional support that is needed to make and to maintain change.

If you review the titles of the first five chapters of *Stop the Sabotage*, you will see that these issues are directly proportionate to the amount of time that you stay in your head without reality testing and support. For example, we are more likely to think that a disproportionate amount of what others think and do is related to us when we don't have a support network to keep us grounded in reality. A support person will tell you that everything is not about you and that people have more important things to do than focus on you. Support is often about staying in the here and now, rather than in the past or future.

We have a choice about those from whom we seek support. Secondly we can ask for the exact type of support we need. We know those well-meaning people who do not know how to support us in the way that works best for us. I see this in a lot of mother/daughter relationships. The daughter will be working on trying to look more attractive or on losing weight and her mom will attempt to be supportive with statements such as, "Honey, did you really want your hair to look that way?" or "You really shouldn't wear that, it is just isn't that slimming". This will probably make the daughter ready to go out and dye her hair pink and eat a box of chocolates. Be aware that you can pick your support system and you can ask for the type of support that you want.

Sometimes you may want a tough friend who will dish out the hard cold facts, especially when the change is a life or death issue. If the doctor tells you that without some behavioral change you will be lucky to live another year, look for a tough and supportive person to help you make those changes. Asking for specific types of support can initially be difficult, but it becomes easier with practice.

If you are looking for someone to support you in stopping the habit of being critical and negative, you must find someone who is not critical and negative. This sounds simple, but people do make some unusual choices when they seek support. An ideal support person can also offer words of wisdom on how they manage to keep positive attitudes and maintain a nonjudgmental stance. We are all tempted to talk negatively about people, but there are those who have the skill and wisdom to steer clear of this activity. There are plenty of people who have accomplished the skill of not taking stock of other people's inventory and who keep their focus on themselves. This is the type of support person that you will most often need.

When people work on changing their problem with taking everything personally, they need to find a support person who doesn't exhibit this characteristic. When they write a behavioral contract, they will state that they need to learn that most things that happen in life are not about them. This is a difficult and time/energy-robbing problem with which to deal. I have served as the support person in helping friends resolve this issue. A good support person will know how to help the person with reality testing. A common myth for the "it's all about me" type is that most decisions people make in his or her workplace and social life are based on them. This is a special breed of paranoia that is fed by fear, insecurity, and a need to be significant. A good support person will help the person see the absurdity of believing that other people are constantly thinking and making decisions based on him or her.

Self-disclosure is an excellent characteristic for selecting a support person. In the aforementioned example, a grounded support person will state that the person's boss and co-workers seldom think about him or her. They have their own personal lives and their own work to do. As long as everyone shares the workload and performs well, they do not have to spend any time and energy wondering about how and what others are thinking or saying.

The parenting class that I teach at the homeless shelter is located near a metro stop. I frequently use an example of finding something that is going where you are going and getting on board. If a shelter resident has a job interview in Silver Spring, Maryland, they have a number of options to get there. The fastest and most economical way would be to walk three blocks to the metro. The train will take them to Silver Spring and they only transfer trains once. This trip from Alexandria, Virginia would cost about $4 and would take between 40 and 50 minutes. A cab would cost much more and wouldn't save any time. Walking would take many hours.

The point here is that we need to find something that is going in the same direction that we wish to go and use this vehicle to get there. Real life vehicles that are going our way are everywhere. There are many types of organizations, churches, support groups and many other vehicles for change. Once you identify the changes that you want to make, take a close look at this valuable support piece.

We are living among people, things and events that are moving. For those of us with children living under our roof, we know that they are constantly growing, changing, progressing and being challenged by life. Although children take a great deal of time and energy, I have observed that parents seem less stuck and are more malleable to change while children are in the home. Perhaps this is because they have a vehicle for change with their own children moving and progressing.

Children cause us to adapt to different circumstances and events. Children teach us how to prioritize our lives. The priority of allowing children the options of participating in the arts, sports, and other activities often combats the parent's self-centeredness. Naturally these aren't reasons to have children, but this is one of many positive ways to frame parenthood.

There are a lot of good support groups out there and finding others who are working through the same problem can be a real asset. Going back to the earlier chapter, our support network helps to keep us from getting stuck in the rut of blemishing others and their ideas. It is important to realize that you can always find something in what others say—regardless of whether we agree with them completely. Sift through and take what you can use. Keep an open mind about ideas and concepts you do not agree with. Sometimes we grow into these things much in the same way as a child grows into an older sibling's clothing.

At times it may be best to find one particular person who is an expert in making the change that you wish to make. For example, if your change involves exercise, a personal trainer can be very beneficial. Although this type of support has an expense attached, sometimes the cost will keep us active in our exercise program. People have told me that the primary reason that they show up at the gym is that they have an appointment with a trainer. Also, people tend to value those things that they pay for. This is also true for hiring a registered dietician or a life coach.

Twelve step programs have been using a great idea for many decades: the use of a sponsor. This is a person who has been in the program for a while and who knows the program very well. They are familiar with the steps and traditions of the program and offer support as often as needed. The idea of a sponsor has caught on and is now used in many areas of recovery and personal growth.

The ideal sponsor, mentor, or any other person who will support you in a structured fashion, will set limits for you. For example, you cannot constantly tell a good support person about your past wounds and expect continued sympathy. You will be reminded that the past cannot be changed and that you do not wish to be identified as "that wounded person" who had been dealt a bad hand earlier in life. Good support people know they aren't helping you by simply hearing all the excuses about why you can't change or that your story is so much more unique than the stories of others. They will take each excuse and counter with insight and wisdom that reality tests each excuse.

We always have a choice of how we frame our quest for change. If we think that it is going to be difficult and take a long time, it will be both. If our mother and father were overweight and we are genetically pre-disposed to be fat, a good support person will challenge this thinking because he or she will know that thoughts have power over your outcome.

The lack of eliciting support is one of the major reasons people fail to make and to maintain change. Think about those times when you failed and then determine whether the lack of support was one of the reasons for failure. If so, you now know what to do differently.

Looking, Acting and Feeling Different

The contractual question here is, "How will you look, act, and feel differently after you have made the change that you are working on?" Another part of this question is to think about how others will perceive you as being different. Since we do not know, nor can we control, how others perceive anything, this is a speculative question. However it is worth asking. This step in the change process is really one of vision.

The primary question is one that fits well into your initial cost/benefit analysis. Many people do not ask this question prior to embarking upon change. During my many years as a therapist, I would ask clients to close their eyes and imagine that they had made their target change. I would ask how they would look, act, and feel differently after they had achieved the goal(s) for which they had sought therapy. Next, I would ask them to describe a scene where they would most exhibit this change and to talk about this scene. They would explore how they would look and describe this in detail. They would describe how they moved, interacted, and how they felt. This gave them a glimpse into their future and offered a rewarding memory of the future on which to build.

As you can imagine, some clients would look at me as if I had two heads when I asked them to undertake this visualization. If someone is not in touch with the personal outcome of a change, this can present problems. The inability to think or feel about the end product of a change process can definitely impact one's cost/benefit analysis.

While working on my Masters in Social Work degree, I worked in a therapeutic community for drug addicts. I recall telling a new resident during her first few week of residential treatment, "When you see yourself as I can see now, you will be ready to graduate." She eventually did see her strengths and, after graduation from the program, became very successful.

At times, you may know someone who sees something in you that you cannot see in yourself. If this is true, ask this person what he or she sees and on what they base their observation. You may be able to begin to see this vision of yourself. Sometimes a shared visualization is one way to kick-start your visions of your future self.

Visualization is not a new technique. We often hear about athletes who see themselves catching the ball, running across the goal line, jumping the hurdle, lifting the weight or completing the perfect skating routine. Mental rehearsal is a valid way of seeing yourself achieving your goals. I use this when giving important speeches or prior to filming an interview. This technique has always served me well.

I remember my first TV appearance in 1981 on a local talk show. The host interviewed me about the best ways to prevent white-collar crime. Although I had lectured extensively on the topic of preventing white-collar crime through attitude change, I had not been publicly interviewed on this topic. I recall mentally rehearsing prior to the show. When the show began, I felt as if the host and I were sitting in my living room without the TV cameras.

When presenting information to fitness professionals and clients, I often talk about how imagery can assist someone to claim an exercise environment as their own personal domain. When one enters a gym or exercise room and he or she feels competent, in control and approval, the environment will be comfortable and not intimidating. Visualize Emeril Lagasse in the kitchen—his domain. Your goal is to make places where wellness occurs in your domain.

Visualization can be as useful as rehearsal for upcoming events. It will allow you to get in touch with some of the many fears that can exist regarding making change. Some fears are apparent while others are hidden from us in layers of personal defense mechanisms. Although some people are striving for a better body image and a more outgoing personality, they may discover fears when they explore life after these changes occur. A woman may fear being seen solely as a sex object or a man may fear being expected to be sociable in a crowd of people with whom he believes he has no common bond. Some people may experience a fear that change will increase other's expectations of them.

I have used the technique of looking at how I would be different after a change. During graduate school, I was working on increasing my self-honesty. In particular, I wanted to curtail my tendency of being overly diplomatic and to say more of what I really thought. As part of my information gathering process I studied principles from reading and listening to the work of well-known sages. One tenet within these teachings was that we are not what we have, what we do, or what others think about us. My goal was to work on the last principle.

Being overly concerned about what others think about us can be maddening. Once we recognize that our reputation is something external from us, we can appreciate the powerlessness we have over our reputation. Once we reach the point of being the best person that we can be, we come closer to living in harmony with kindness, love, acceptance and other universal thoughts and feelings. At this point, we can stop worrying about what others think of us.

Working on how others will see you will take care of itself once you have embraced the daily goal of always doing the next right thing. Caring what others think of you can take a lot of time and energy; the outcomes can vary. Our reputation is independent from us and is dependent on what others think of us.

Having read 12-step recovery books, I looked at the true meaning of "letting go and letting God " (or whatever entity you believe to be larger than yourself). It is important to be clear about the fact that not everyone will like us. Once we realize that the goal of always doing the next right thing is the best we can do, the majority of people will always like us if they really know us. This daily effort can eliminate our fear of personal, malicious or mean-spirited behavior on our part. When we think about this, these negative characteristics really aren't part of most of our personalities.

Tabloid headlines frequently reveal that people performed unlawful acts as teens or young adults, or question the sexual preference of celebrities. Regardless of the validity of such statements, why should anyone really care? One can't help think of that old Bible verse that says, "Let those among us without sin cast the first stone."

To test my growth in not focusing on what others think of me, I use imagery. I picture myself in a grocery store checkout lane reading a tabloid headline about myself. On the front page, I see a 1974 police photo taken of me after being picked up on a fugitive from justice warrant for escaping from jail. The headline states, "Self-help Author and Speaker's Criminal Past Revealed." I picture myself looking at the tabloid, picking it up and people saying, "That is you." I then calmly respond, "Yes, this is me." As I speak, I don't feel any urge to defend myself or to explain the article. I feel complete peace and serenity.

This imagery worked. I realized that I could reach the point where I would actually be at peace and not care what others thought. As long as I get out of bed each day and go about doing the next right thing, I really do not care what others think of me. I have been able to share this with others who are working on the same issue and they report that it has been extremely helpful. As you think about looking at how you will look, act, and feel differently after your change has occurred, you may wish to consider using this type of imagery.

Life has a way of presenting us with events that allow us to test our growth. One day, while casually dressed, a lady asked me if I had found a job. We were riding the Metro through Alexandria, Virginia toward the District of Columbia. She had seen me at a homeless shelter where I co-teach a parenting class. She assumed I lived there. I simply answered her question by saying I had found a job and wished her a good day. I didn't feel any desire to explain to her I didn't live in the shelter. This was a sign of personal growth. The fact that people live in a homeless shelter doesn't define who they are.

Prior to completing your internal cost/benefit analysis, I recommend pursuing this step of imagining how you will look, act, and feel differently after you have made and maintained your target change. Sometimes the imagery will give you that extra incentive to pursue your change with clear determination and the knowledge that your targeted change will be worth the effort.

An interesting paradox of working on this step of the contract is that you may find that you are improving your self-image from the very first day. This step requires the courage of introspection. You will discover that you are using the higher energy thoughts and emotions of the acceptance of self and of others. This look into your future allows you to use your imagination.

I frequently use the following quote from Albert Einstein: "Imagination is more important than knowledge. For knowledge is limited to all we now know and understand, while imagination embraces the entire world and all there will ever be to know and understand." For those who have left their imagination in their childhood, this step of the change contract can revitalize the power of imagination as a guiding force in our lives.

As a sidebar to this individual process, I have noted that groups and organizations can benefit greatly from discussing how they will look, act, and feel differently after they have made target changes. As someone who reviews human service organizations for accreditation, the attempts at change that seem to fail most often are those where a clear vision for the future has not been developed.

Personal Sabotages

The next question is, "How may you sabotage your change efforts?" By the time people take the initiative to read a book about making and maintaining change, they will have encountered some degree of failure. I pose that most people can make an initial change, but fail in maintaining the change. Personal sabotages are the key reason for failure. Up to this point, I have discussed quite a few categories of personal sabotages. Among them have been the following:

- Discounting information
- Inefficient structure and use of time
- Fears and insecurities
- Judgmental attitudes
- Poor use of personal energy
- Not completing a thorough cost/benefit analysis
- Not seeking support and not asking for the specific support that you need

- Believing your ego's message that you are separate from others and not part of something much larger than yourself

If any of the above issues fit you, specifically identify exactly how these and/or other issues have sabotaged your efforts to improve your life. Go back and re-read the chapter(s) that pertains to you. This investment in time will be beneficial and may put you on a track of performing a more honest cost/benefit analysis for your target change.

You are the ultimate expert on yourself. Take time to look at why you have failed in the past. Be brutally honest. Sometimes sabotages are easily identifiable; however, many of them require some introspection. As we age, we tend to see patterns. If relationships have failed for 40 years or if an inordinate number of subordinate employees have quit or threatened to quit under your supervision, this is a good sign that it is not entirely their fault.

It is a good idea to learn more about your personality. There are plenty of revealing tests that can help you realize more about your personality and your preferences. The Myers-Briggs® and the Enneagram® are excellent tests that you can research. Tests can help you make an informed decision about whether the results would help you identify some of your sabotaging behaviors. We frequently swim upstream against our personality traits. It is helpful to know when you are doing this and then know how to plan and act accordingly.

I previously mentioned the sabotage of waiting until you have enough information. Although most changes have an information-gathering component, you should limit the time you engage in this process. You can always discover more about any topic. You can always get the opinion of one more person. At times people get tied up in a "be perfect" script and they believe that one more piece of information will somehow make the change a lot easier. No one has all of the available information before embarking on a change. We can work too hard on gaining information about our target change as well as not working hard enough.

Apathy caused by comfort can be a hidden sabotage. Apathy is a very low energy feeling—just above guilt and shame. There is a certain amount of comfort in doing the things that we have always done. This is "the devil you know versus the devil you don't" analogy. Apathy, as with most negative emotions, can often be traced back to fear. Fear to do something different is a common issue. What if you fail? This is a wonderful question to reality test. Part of facing your fear is addressed in the previous step of seeing how you will look, act, and feel differently after you make your change. Sometimes the imagery exercise will allow you to get in touch with fear-based apathy. The willingness to recognize this dynamic can move your forward. I have encountered this apathy/comfort/fear connection both in my clinical work with clients and in working for municipal, state, federal government agencies for decades.

Working for the government has been referred to as wearing the "golden handcuffs" because of the job security and excellent benefits it brings. There comes a point that people become very comfortable with the predictability of government work. At the same time, some government employees dream of going out on their own to pursue their dreams. This is an especially difficult decision when a person has a family. Families with children need good health care and the security of a predictable income. Apathy can occur because, after completing a cost/benefit analysis, the employee decides that the possible benefit of leaving government for a less secure job isn't worth the cost. This is neither good nor bad; it simply is a reality. This is an easily understood example of the relationship between apathy, comfort and fear.

This is also an excellent example of another big sabotage to change—"all or none thinking." This process was discussed in the first chapter when referring to how we are programmed to accept all of a package or ideology or not accept it at all. The all or none thinker doesn't look at simultaneously pursuing goals that take him out of his comfort zone and into areas of personal interest. For example, I know many government workers who simultaneously work home-based businesses, teach college, write and publish articles teach yoga and pursue a multitude of other endeavors while remaining at their government jobs.

If your sabotage is inconsistency, realize that a new behavior must be practiced on many consecutive days before it becomes second nature. Let us look at a few examples. If you have decided to make some lifestyle changes due to early signs of stiffness and immobility in your joints, you may decide to do some stretching exercises and to take glucosamine on a daily basis.

If you already take a daily vitamin or medication, the addition of another pill will probably not be a problem. If you do not currently take medication or supplements, you need to develop a system whereby you take pills on a daily basis. For example, if you make coffee every morning, you can put the pills on the part of the coffee maker that you must open before filling the water well. Be creative!

If your body is becoming less flexible and you have decided to perform a daily stretching routine that takes 12 minutes, these 12 minutes should become part of you daily routine. There is no magic formula to making new routines second nature. Use a scheduling method, a support person to remind you and to follow-up, or a partner who wishes to do the exercise with you. Use any means possible to ensure that the new behavior becomes a part of your life. Without a methodology to ensure consistency, you are sabotaging your success.

If your target behavioral change focuses on quitting a behavior, a major sabotage is to not put something in its place. Old behaviors served a number of purposes: they were part of your structure of time and the old behavior had some sort of accompanying reward. The behavior that you are trying to extinguish may have been associated with socializing with others. It may have been a way to relax or to get your blood pumping. For whatever reason, the old behavior had a function. When it is gone, you will have a void. How will you fill it?

If you have a plan for filling a void before you begin making your change, this is another positive for considering your cost/benefit analysis. Smoking, drinking and risky sexual behavior are a few of the apparent behaviors that people attempt to quit. One aspect that people often overlook about such behaviors is that they fulfill needs and occupy both mental and physical time. One must fill the emotional and time voids left by reducing and then ceasing a behavior.

People work on quitting certain thought patterns. For example, some people may be working on reducing thoughts and feelings related to bitterness and resentments. Although this time-consuming obsession robs us of time and energy, it is difficult to release until we have a replacement strategy. There must be something to slowly fill the void proportionately as these thoughts and feelings slowly subside. One can actually crowd out obsessive thinking with other thoughts and feelings. Many activities have clear accompanying thoughts and feelings. You can explore this principle.

Logic tells us that we should not be reading, listening to and watching things that trigger bitterness and hatred. Staying away from news, talk shows, reality shows, and any program that hooks one's negative emotions is advisable. Instead, watching comedies, the food channel or HGTV may be a safe choice. Some light reading would be good. Craft projects, painting, and gardening all offer ways of creatively using thought and energy. As one becomes more self-assured with new emotions, some of those things that were eliminated can be slowly reintegrated. However, some of these things will be found to be distasteful once the change has been made and maintained for a while.

The key to this step of looking at ways that you could sabotage your change is to look at your previous roadblocks and to realize that you were the cause of the roadblocks. You may find that the sabotages are the first problems to resolve. If so, work at eliminating the sabotages.

Many of the sabotages that I have mentioned can have catastrophic effects on your health and wellbeing. Some are symptoms of serious and sometimes life-threatening problems. Bottled-up hatred, fear, insecurity, resentments and guilt can be exhibited in such sabotages as discounting information and inefficient use of mental time and energy. If these are the root causes of any of your sabotages, change is not only advisable it is necessary for a longer and more productive life. The elimination of these sabotages can be more important than the changes that you originally set out to make. If you find this to be the case, make the sabotage the problem and use the methodology of *Stop the Sabotage* to address it.

While working in a therapeutic community for drug addicts, I observed that people would quit and walk away during two periods of treatment—near the beginning and near the end. It was easy to understand why people left during the beginning of treatment: this was a tough environment with a lot of rules, expectations and confrontation. However, many people would leave toward the end of treatment. Some would be in the 13th to 15th month and others would be in the re-entry phase and could see the light at the end of the tunnel. I interviewed quite a few of these people and asked why they left treatment. Some had already been incarcerated because they were in the treatment program in lieu of going to prison. Many of them said that they left treatment because they were fearful.

During the change process, there comes a time when a person realizes that it is equally as easy to do things the new way as it is to do it the old way. While socializing with others away from the program, residents would realize that they could have a good time without getting high and this was now a real choice for them. The entire notion of choice was new to them and this type of choice was frightening. This choice meant living responsibly and doing the next right thing.

Although most of you are not struggling with the level of change faced by the recovering heroin addict, be aware that fear is often normal when a choice is first apparent. This is something to address during the visualization exercise. Many changes require a level of self-confidence and the self-assurance that you will be okay when making a new and less familiar choice.

Building on
Past Success

The last step of the change contract entails looking at your previous successes and drawing a frame of reference from these successes. This step can be done at the beginning, especially when you do not believe that you have a substantial track record of success in making personal changes. As we identify our sabotages for past failures, we can also identify our successes. Successes, once identified, may not appear to have any relationship to the things that you are currently working to change. However, they do relate; success is success and all success has common threads.

I frequently see this success factor in the world of business. People who possess a history of excellent management skills will go into a business in which they know very little. If they learn quickly, they learn the ins and outs of any type of business. However, it is their management skills that translate well into their leadership position. Their knowledge and skill transcends many types of business.

You have learned skills and have used these skills to resolve problems, to overcome obstacles, and to make and maintain change. It is up to you to identify these skills and processes. Sometimes you must first identify a life event where you did well. Remember that personal successes often occur during the most difficult times in life. Success can occur during some of your darkest days and are often interpreted as simply surviving a difficult situation. During these types of circumstances, we tend to frame our successes as simply doing what had to be done—as the right thing to do.

I have heard people relate great successes while living in foster care, while incarcerated, or in the midst of a difficult divorce. While working for the US Department of Veterans Affairs, I heard success stories of coping and survival that were truly amazing. These successes are sometimes buried in surviving and in carrying out the responsibilities of daily living. Take some time to identify and explore the component parts of your past successes. Identify what worked and why it worked. Then look at the common denominators that apply to the change that you are now pursuing.

One common characteristic that is often overlooked or minimized is the ability to stay focused during a crisis. When I see people go through the death of a friend or family member, I notice that they are focused on making sure that each detail is meticulously carried out. They attend to those who need support and they are extremely dependable throughout the entire difficult ordeal. This type of focus, empathy, and tenacity can be generalized to many of life's challenges.

A person who has been an average parent has a record of success in many areas. Regardless of the era in which you may have parented children, each era had special problems that had to be overcome. Parenting requires persistence and always involves some level of sacrifice. There are those times when parents want their child to act differently than they have modeled for them and they make personal changes to better model positive behavior. Parenting requires setting aside some portion of selfishness and taking a utilitarian view of life. Parents learn to make long-range plans and to prioritize based on the needs of others.

While teaching a parenting class, I learned the importance of modeling for children and for other parents. On occasion, there are not any volunteers to watch the children and my co-teacher and I are in a room full of parents and small children. We both function well in the chaos, as do many of the parents. It is during these classes that I often see the strengths of the parents that allow me to know that they will do well after leaving the shelter. I witness the quiet concern and guidance that can be generalized to many of life's problems and that is an intricate part of many change processes. We make a point of drawing attention to the strengths that we see and focus on how well the parents' function within the chaos.

I worked with a middle-age male during my time as a therapist at a public mental health clinic. He had been briefly treated for depression and suicidal ideation in one of the state psychiatric hospitals. The change that he was working on was increasing his self-concept so that he would have the confidence to grow his small janitorial business. He basically related that he did not have any interpersonal skills or frame-of-reference to draw upon. During one session we discussed his time in prison for multiple check forgery charges.

In the course of this man's incarceration he was president of the Jaycee chapter, won a number of awards in leadership and public speaking, was a member of the Great Books Cub, taught other men how to read, and accomplished a plethora of other notable contributions to that community. He had written these successes off because they occurred in prison. We explored these accomplishments and their component parts. I asked him if he could relate these past successes to his current life. He was able to draw from these successes and moved on to accomplish his goals.

This may seem like an extreme situation, but it makes my point that successes can be found amid the most difficult times. I can relate many cases of welfare-to-work mothers who once lived on Temporary Assistance for Needy Families (TANF) and other public assistance programs who have drawn from past successes to accomplish the changes that they desired. I have met women who are currently attorneys, child welfare administrators, and city managers that have risen from public assistance to become highly successful leaders.

When working on chapter 8 (Developing and Utilizing Support), I asked people to relate if someone within their support network had assisted them in realizing their strengths. Those who answered "yes" related that friends or family saw strengths that they had not seen. The question that you may wish to ask yourself is whether you should candidly ask about what others see as your strengths.

I previously mentioned a very fragile person during her first month of long-term drug treatment and that she would be ready to leave treatment when see saw her strengths as clearly as I saw them. Upon her graduation from the therapeutic community, she commented on my words and stated that this was indeed the secret for her success. She grew to trust my words as she worked with me and began believing in her strengths. Realizing strengths is often a gradual process.

Take a lesson from how you learned to read. Remember how you learned words and then how to form words into sentences and then into paragraphs. If you learned a second language, remember how that process occurred. We learn many of our most difficult lessons in very small increments that are "baby steps—putting one step in front of the other." Some changes require this sort of process. Repeating these small steps can accomplish great things. Ponder your history of learning and changing through using this type of exposure. The tenacity that comes with slowly developing skills is reinforced if we take time to appreciate our forward movement and our increasing capacity to change.

A common term used in human services is "capacity building". An organization's ability to build increased capacity to serve more consumers or to serve them more effectively is a challenge. However many organizations have learned how to do more with less and how to assist the consumer with advocating for themselves. Excellent organizations have learned how to utilize volunteers and coordinate services with other providers.

In teaching a class on the topic of continuous quality improvement, I have struggled to find personal examples of capacity building. One that I use is to explain that I have been a personal trainer for 16 years and thus know the biomechanics of exercise. I know multiple ways to work each muscle group. When I go to the gym during my lunch hour, I have a limited time to exercise. Because of the crowd, I cannot always access my first or second choice of equipment. However, through formal training and experience, I have the capacity to use machines, cables, free weights, or my body weight to work may target muscle groups.

Person trainers can assist a client with building capacity to use multiple pieces of equipment to work a muscle group. Therapist, counselors, and yogi instructors can assist clients in increasing their capacity to deal with stress. Many of the changes that we pursue are really about building our capacity to thrive in difficult times.

Individuals have learned how to build their capacity to do more with less. This is often a strength that is overlooked. Take a look at how you have learned to be more efficient with your resources and give yourself credit for your success. Efficiency in time, energy, money or any resource is a big plus for any change that you wish to make. With the unemployment rate hovering around 10 percent, many people are building the capacity to do more with less. Once life circumstances improve, the capacity built during hard times will remain a strength on which to build future successes.

Chapter 8, "Developing and Utilizing Support", is in many ways about building personal capacity through interpersonal relationships. The development of a supportive social network is a form of personal capacity building. The utilization of social networking sites that focus on career building is a form of capacity building.

Use the change contract for yourself to build your capacity for change. Give considerable thought to each step and make notes to yourself. Make it a living contract that you can track and alter when necessary. You will learn more about yourself than you may have thought possible. Keep a record of your progress.

The following section will focus on ways to augment your change process. I am offering additional tools to ensure your ability to make and to maintain your personal change.

Using Symbols, Action and Ritual to Enhance Change

Many people spend an inordinate amount of time and money on attending motivational and inspirational workshops and listening to similar material on various audio and video formats. I have done this for decades. However information alone does not keep change going. Most people leave a motivational speech feeling motivated and have a few new ideas about how to keep a can-do attitude. However, when they arise the next morning the change is only a vague memory and they go back to their reality.

The use of symbols is one concrete way to keep the image and intent of change alive within us. Symbols can be an omnipresent reminder of where we are going and how we will get there. Symbols paired with action and ritual give us a winning combination of making continuous improvements in life. Let us begin with exploring symbols.

We are surrounded by symbols. The same symbol can elicit different feelings from different people. When many of us see the swastika of the Third Reich our blood runs cold. When we see a decorative flag on a home of a stork carrying a baby we feel joy because we know that the family is celebrating a birth. Take some time and think about the most meaningful symbols in your life and ask yourself why these are meaningful. Symbols can be as personal and unique as our DNA or as ubiquitous as the Apple Logo. Regardless, the use of symbols can be a powerful tool for maintaining change and for achieving continuous progress in life.

Because we have five senses, I have an expanded definition of symbols. Although we most frequently define a symbol as something visual, I define a symbol as anything that arouses one or more of the senses and has a representational meaning. For example, when I smell peaches, I think of my grandmother because her house often had that aroma during the summer. She represented unconditional love and patience.

The advent of the iPod has made it easy to develop playlists of our favorite music. I have developed a play list of my favorite workout tunes and play these tunes on days when I need a boost to keep myself on the path to fitness. I can listen to tunes from Rocky IV and feel motivation to keep going. My wife and I go to sleep each night listening to the sound of ocean waves. The sound of the waves takes us to a beach house on the ocean far away from work and daily responsibilities.

When I hear particular songs, I think of particular times, places and people; some of these are strong symbols for change. Songs in particular seem to cause many of us to recall days past or what some refer to as "the good old days." Each generation seems to have an affinity for the popular music of its youth—back when music seemed to have an added meaning. There is some paradox in listening and remembering our era's music. Yes, we can enjoy the memories, but we cannot return to the past.

Do you find yourself activating one of your senses for the purpose of changing your mood? Do you use symbols to remind you where you are going? If so, there is a strong likelihood that symbols will be useful in making and maintaining a change that you are working on.

Symbols can represent the past, the present and the future. Some symbols represent all three. I have a poster of the New York skyline over my desk at work. This picture is representative of having spent quite of bit of my life in New York. I love the city and I have great admiration for its people and their resolve during times of adversity. The picture also reminds me each day of moving forward. Because I have scheduled trips to New York for conferences and meetings, I use the picture to focus on upcoming events.

Take some time to think about symbols that motivate you. For example, pictures that remind you of good times that you want to replicate can be useful. For those who use symbols as metaphors, this has the potential to greatly expand your use of symbols. A good example of a metaphorical use of a symbol is a picture of a musical instrument. Although you may not play an instrument, you may have heard the statement that people should not die with their music still in them. The metaphor of music refers to one's dreams that can be fulfilled during life by using one's skills, abilities and talents. Thus, the picture of an instrument or printed music will remind you to pursue your life's destiny. Also, listening to music can be a reminder of the same goal.

Symbols can also represent a process. The Annie E. Casey Foundation developed videos about their Family-to-Family Program. One video, about the process of family group conferencing, refers to building bridges between families and the community. Throughout the video there are pictures of bridges. Thus, the bridge has become a personal symbol for me that relates to building relationships between individuals and families, families and extended families, and families and communities.

If you have ever designed a business card or advertisement logo from an array of photographs, drawings and clip art, you have seen many symbols that represent processes. When I developed knightsjourney.org during 2002, I focused on symbols that represent a journey. Some of the items I selected were lighthouses, maps, a lamp to represent knowledge, and a sextant to represent guidance. As I put this large website together, the symbols held the themes together and continued to keep me focused on my goals and objectives for this site.

Sometimes you may need to change the symbols in your life. As we change, so should our symbols. I have focused therapy on the process of giving up an old symbol and replacing it with another. People will give up status symbols for symbols of peace and tranquility. This is common among those who move from urban areas into rural areas. Some young people give up symbols of death and fatalism for symbols of life and hope. You may find it useful to see whether you keep any nonproductive or useless symbols in your life.

I find it useful to replace some symbols with others. The success of this process depends on whether the letting go of one symbol and the adoption of another means a change in attitude or philosophy as well. For example, if you want to give up a monster-size, eight cylinder, gas-guzzling SUV because you realize that you want to do your part in conserving fuel or because you no longer want a tank-like vehicle to survive a possible crash; you may want to replace it with a reasonably economical and safe SUV or car. This is more than changing your vehicle; it is a shift in attitude and philosophy that can have ramifications in other parts of your life.

If a stranger came into your home and closely observed each room, what would they discover about you? When invited to a stranger's home by way of my wife's friends and business associates, I purposely see how much I can learn about our host by looking at the décor. What I often see in some homes are very clear symbols of where the person has been, where they are, and where they are going. In doing this I have correctly deduced future successes and failures in personal lives and in business.

Consider the symbols that will help you to stay focused on the goals and objectives of the change that you are working on. Sometimes these are pictures that are readily available. I have recommended to clients that they make a collage of pictures from magazines. This project is one that forces thought about the significance of symbols. Make an effort to experiment with using symbols to make and to maintain change. Be creative!

One common dominator in how world religions have continued through the centuries is the use of action and specific rituals. Rituals are action oriented and become symbolic over time. When emotions and feelings combine with thoughts, we have a recipe for continual and self–perpetuated motion. As long as our emotions are driven by love rather than hate and fear, the symbolism of deliberate action motivates us toward similar actions.

Action takes the theoretical and makes it real. Pairing symbols with action and ritual makes for a recipe for success. If a person is striving towards an increase in their cardiovascular fitness they must exercise the heart. Watching a video about the danger of heart disease and the laurels of exercise will not suffice. If we get out of bed, drink 20 ounces of water and jump on the treadmill for 20 minutes every morning, this is a ritual and puts action into the change equation.

If we are striving to spend our life doing what we love and get paid for it, we first need to do more of what we know best. If you are a good musician and you would like to play music for a living, what are you doing? Are you practicing every day, playing publicly and with others at every opportunity? Have you made a CD of your best work and have it available either for free or for sale? Have you identified and developed those personal characteristics that set you apart from others? All of these are actions steps. Practicing, writing music, and making yourself open to learning successful methods to live your dream must become ritual.

A person interested in fashion design that possesses the basic skills may watch the video "Unzipped" about designer Isaac Mizrahi. He or she may be inspired by this story, but then lose motivation. If the person, while motivated, takes pencil in hand and sketches a few ideas or cuts a pattern that never got cut—they are applying action to the idea. Calling over a few friends, getting feedback, making a dress, coat, pair of pants and putting them on just the right person and seeing the result may be just the ticket to gaining more motivation.

Spend some quality time with yourself deciding how to put the symbols that you need in your life. Remember that each of your senses respond to symbols. Don't think too long; get started today.

Staying in
the Flow

One summer, a friend and I took a fishing trip on a rubber raft down the Shenandoah River. The water was crystal clear and I could frequently see the rocky bottom. We could see the fish from quite a distance. The river was fairly calm with only a few small rapids. As we floated down the river I thought about the change process.

It dawned on me that this river experience would be a wonderful venue for teaching lessons about making and maintaining change. I would be assured that my students would be extremely clear on the most salient points. Also, this river experience would make it easy to make the leap from maintaining change to making continuous progress in life.

The raft and the river were perfect teaching examples with the raft being the individual and the river representing life. Life has a flow, like the current of the river. There are obstacles such as the shallow rapids that must be navigated with care. The people in the raft can simply move with the flow and give slight direction to the raft, but the primary movement is caused by the natural flow of the river.

Recognizing the flow of life is perhaps the most challenging obstacle for us. Some people will paddle up-stream and against the current much of the time. They deplete their time and energy to no great end. We all know those who do this from childhood until death without any clue that life could have been easier and more rewarding.

The past is the water that you have traveled, the future is down-river (the place you are going) and the present is where the raft is now. What better example states the importance of being in the "now"? It is now that we develop and nurture relationships and build our capacity to thrive in our environment. Most importantly, it is now that we unplug from our ego and plug into all of the abundance that surrounds us.

The river is what it is and not what you wish it to be; it is neither good nor bad. We can reframe the river as much as we wish; it remains a river and it doesn't care about our titles and descriptions. A river doesn't have an ego. When we compare ourselves with others, feel insecure and fearful, and wish to change the external world, it continues to flow along and we are left asking many "why" questions and making "if only" statements. We become stuck in our thoughts instead of simply appreciating and feeling gratitude for life with its abundance of beauty, serenity, and wisdom. It is easy to detach from self-centered thinking when you are ridding with the flow of the water. While on the river, we don't try to make sense of it any more than we should make sense out of that which has neither apparent reason nor logic.

If this description of flowing along with life sounds remotely familiar, it very well may be. This is a Zen principle. Zen is neither a religion nor a philosophy. It is a way of experiencing the liberation of the mind and a method to unplug from all of the unhealthy characteristics mentioned throughout *Stop the Sabotage* such as fear-based emotion. The practice of mindfulness also augments our ability to stay in the present. The practice of these principles can greatly assist in keeping us in the flow rather that going against the current.

As a social work graduate student I recall being taught a key element of psychosocial casework—"start where the client is." I found this to be an invaluable piece of information. Good information that can help one to make positive changes should be written in such a way that one may see where they are. If we use the river analogy, the question is, "Where are you on the river?" Are you stuck in some trees along the edge or are you caught in the rapids and holding on for dear life? Are you paddling against the current?

Everyone is on a continuum of personal growth. Hopefully one's place on this continuum advances with age. As the following story indicates, many years with one company are not necessarily a sign that one has learned to recognize and to go with the flow of life.

Prior to beginning college, I worked in retail management. After completing the management-training program in a large retail store, I was transferred to work as an assistant manager in a small store in metropolitan Washington, D.C. My former manager was a dynamo and had been transferred to Georgia to manage the entire southern region of the company. My new manager had begun working for the company at the same time and in the same Baltimore store as my former manager.

One was now a regional manager and the other was the manager of a small store. In speaking with my former manager about why his and my current manager's paths were so different, he posed an important question. He asked me what it meant if a person had worked for a company for 20 years. My answer began with the importance of experience and the important factors of developing a successful leadership and management style. He allowed me to go on for a while before stopping me.

He finally told me an important truth. "The only thing that this means is that the person has worked for the same company for 20 years—nothing else". Fortunately he didn't explain this in any great detail, allowing me to seek the meaning of his statement. It is true that experience can teach a great deal. However, experience can also mean that a person has been going in the wrong direction for decades.

I have realized that many of those who have advanced and are excellent in their profession have learned the flow of life. They haven't spent their time and energy blaming external forces for all that is wrong. They take responsibility for their mistakes, learn from them and move forward. They aren't dogmatic and know that life's answers can come from anyone at anytime and in any place. These are people who have unplugged themselves from negativity and have plugged into the guiding forces of love, compassion, and doing the next right thing. They honor all life with its abundance while fully realizing that life is not all about them.

In these times of increasingly peculiar weather patterns, you may think of my river analogy and consider both flooding and drought. A river can have too much water to stay within its' banks or it can become a dry riverbed. At times our lives are flooded with people, events and circumstances. At other times, our lives may seem dry and desolate. We seem to suffer from lack of physical, emotional and spiritual nourishment.

Life often seems as if we are flooded when our plates are too full. It is OK to keep one's plate full as long as it has the right content for the right reason. The natural flow of life will allow us to keep our plates as full as we wish if we are doing so for all of the right reasons. Because the energy expended on positive and productive endeavors allow us to prosper and grow, our plates grow. By letting go of our criticisms about people, places and things that we cannot change, ineffective uses of time and energy, and throwing away the garbage in our heads, our plates will have increased capacity. I have seen this happen repeatedly. This is a natural and logical reward of not swimming up stream, but rather going with the flow of life.

Over the years, I have been asked about the relationship between the speeds that one travel through life and the natural flow of life. There is a logical, intentional, and rational pace for each of us. Speed is not a necessity to accomplish more. Some have learned that we must slow down to go faster and to accomplish more. By faster, I simply mean knowing how to stay focused with a clarity that best accompanies being in the flow of life. Speed is seldom analogous with clarity of intent and action.

Speed depletes us of our serenity without which we make an increasing number of mistakes. Since life is more about listening than talking and more about being open than being closed to our surroundings, we suffer from speed. Would you enjoy a gourmet meal if you gobbled it down as you would a burger from the drive thru on the way to an appointment for which you are late? Would you or your child enjoy that bedtime story as much if you read as fast as possible? Speed is good when it is a requirement or it enables you to win a race, but speed shouldn't be a choice when options are available. Most of the time, speed is like blame and bigotry—it is toxic.

Expand the areas that you consider to be your domain until life is your domain. If you are uncomfortable with going somewhere that you wish to go, master this domain and call it yours. Many older people and those who are in poor physical shape do not enjoy going to the gym because they don't feel comfortable. While completing graduate research, I looked at this issue and discovered that people who could learn to feel competence, control, and approval while at the gym would be more likely to go on a regular basis.

Those who initially worked with a personal trainer who was sensitive to the client's issues were able to feel mastery of this environment and thus felt a level of control while in the gym. They then developed self-approval and approval also came from external sources. Thus the gym became part of the person's domain. This type of process can be generalized to many other processes and places.

One of the key points about making and maintaining change is to use repetition. Using the river analogy, the river is repetitive in its motion as are the tides in the ocean. For a new behavior to become secondary, it should be practiced for 21 consecutive days. Repetition is the key to maintaining even very small changes. If you decide to begin taking a vitamin each day, repetition will make this a permanent habit. Symbols can remind people to perform a daily task. Use refrigerator magnets, pictures, and symbols to keep yourself on track. Refer back to the chapter about using symbols. Use meaningful music to remind and to motivate you to stay on track.

One important way of learning about the natural flow of life is to spend some time in nature. This doesn't mean that you must go to the mountains to hike or camp. Manhattan and most urban areas have parks. Natural surroundings are everywhere. In nature you often find the feeling of connectedness that represents the lessons from my trip down the river.

Another lesson from floating down the river was that water is very strong. However, it is extremely malleable. It is the flow of the water that has worn down the rocky bottom of the river over many centuries. People who can have a resilient and malleable state seem to not let life get the best of them. They let the on-coming negative energy flow through and around them. They don't try to resist force with force. If you have ever watched the trees during a strong wind, you will see a good example of this principle.

In the first chapter I stated that we could think about gratitude when our ego starts to rule us and that gratitude and our ego can't occupy the same space. What I didn't say was that trying to fight our own ego is a losing proposition. Trying to overcome our own ego is paddling up-stream. It is best to simply sit back and observe our ego and recognize it for what it is—a self-made fantasy that we have built about ourselves.

As you go about working on those changes that you believe that you must make in order to live a happier and more fulfilling life, remember the principles of flowing with life. You innately have the means by which to make and to maintain any change that you wish to make.

Realize the natural flow of life and that everything has a purpose. Know that everything that occurs in life has the potential to be the best thing that has every happened to you. Live by the rule that you will always do the next right thing and never justify doing less. Your best contribution to society is to be the most authentic person that you can be. With this will come the knowledge both of who you really are, and your life's destiny.

14 The Next Level

I struggled with whether to add this chapter to a book about how to maintain change. My initial thought was to write a second book about this next level. It seems that people are constantly looking for shortcuts or a magic bullet. They want to purchase an abdominal machine that will give them washboard abs in 10 minutes a day or purchase a bottle of pills that will take the weights off and keep it off forever. Such old sayings as "we must crawl before the walk" and "there isn't any substitute for hard work and tenacity" seem appropriate here as I write about "The Next Level"—with the optimal word being "next."

It is true that some get-rich-quick schemes work for a few and that some people have made a You-Tube video and quickly made a fortune due to rapid mass exposure to their talent. These things do happen. However, these stories are the exception and not the rule. I believe that most of us succeed in life by showing up, working toward our goals, and helping as many people as possible along the way. Clarifying our goals and values while being the most genuine people we can be is a clear path to happiness.

Thus, the next level is exactly that—the next place to strive for after you have spent time and effort with successfully maintaining change. For me, it worked after I had mastered the ability to maintain personal change for approximately two decades. Had the next step come along any earlier, I doubt that I would have recognized it for what it was. I don't believe that I would have connected the dots.

Almost a decade ago, I became aware of a concept that takes maintaining change one-step further. This process is continuous quality improvement (CQI). When I began reviewing human service organizations for the Council on Accreditation, I learned that CQI was the key standard to assure organizational excellence. Although this is process that is typically associated with organizational improvement, it is very applicable to small groups, and individuals. My awareness of the path to the next level was quite interesting.

While interviewing a recent college graduate, during an accreditation site visit of a large non-profit social service provider, I was amazed at something she said. When questioning her about her knowledge of the organization's CQI program, she stated, "if I could run my life as well as this agency runs its operation, I know that I would forever be happy and successful; I would continuously me moving forward with my life." This was the first time that I truly appreciated the true personal power of CQI.

Within 8 months of hearing this statement, I was lecturing at national human services conferences on how to get employee buy-in to an organizational CQI program. Because many human service organizations did not have CQI programs, the personalization of CQI was a stretch of some audiences. The exception was the National Conference of COA. The CQI standard, now called

PQI (Performance Quality Improvement) by COA is well known throughout accredited organizations. Participants at this conference know about CQI and are always open to how to improve the process. Thus I had a perfect audience to deliver my message of personal growth through CQI.

There are two key points to be made about continual improvement. First of all, people need an experiential frame-of-reference for maintaining change. They need to have successfully experienced this process so that they have entered a loop of self-reinforcement. This means that their personal on-going process feeds personal success. As one begins to succeed in maintaining change, this success is paired with previous feelings of success and thus the process is easier each time.

Through maintaining change we develop the ability to identify and then to eliminate the sabotages that stop us in our tracks. We then learn a frame-of-reference of successfully maintaining change and learn to make many areas of life "our personal domain." Maintaining change becomes more easily generalized to new areas of change. A long-term consequence is that there is less of a focus of maintaining change and more of a feeling of making continual improvement.

Secondly, and equally important, one must have a frame-of-reference for continual progress. At one time, I believed that everyone had this frame-of-reference. I serendipitously learned this wasn't the case. I could discern, while presenting at national conferences, that some participants didn't have a clue about what I meant by making continuous progress in life. Then I discovered why this was occurring.

Because I travel a great deal and because I am a member of Toastmasters International, I designed a 5 to 7 minute speech to give at Toastmasters' clubs that I visit. My speech topic was, "Making Continual Progress in Life." This was an inspirational and motivational speech and made the point the Toastmasters can serve as a personal frame of reference for continual improvement in life. There was a point in the speech that I would ask my audience "what is your frame of reference of making continual improvement in life?" The audience would always yell out "Toastmasters!"

This speech was so successful that I decided to turn it into a contest speech and give it back home in the metropolitan DC area. I gave this speech and won at the club level and then at the area level. Next I competed it at the division level at the US Department of Education. I got to the audience question and asked, "what is your frame of reference for continuous improvement if life?" The room was totally silent. I looked out at a sea of blank faces, waited a few seconds and then I yelled-out "Toastmasters!" I ended the speech and sat down. Although I won 2nd place, I had learned a lesson that was priceless. Not everyone had a frame-of-reference for making continual improvement. My brief explanation wasn't sufficient for anyone to understand the principles.

In analyzing what had happened that day, I realized that almost everyone in the audience (including me) either worked for the government or a government contractor. Continual improvement isn't really in the lexicon of government work and a brief explanation will not change that fact. I finally understood why I had so many people at national conferences look confused when I presented this topic. A discussion of continual improvement should link with the audience member's previous experience.

Because the Toastmasters methodology does have many inherent characteristics of traditional CQI, most members have a fame of reference for continual improvement.

This organization has a structure for advancing through levels of both leadership and public speaking. Toastmasters offer a roadmap for success. Because every speech is evaluated using evaluation criteria, participants improve with each speech. Leadership projects also include peer feedback.

Practice without feedback sometimes takes us down the road of becoming worse rather than better. Feedback can be internal and/ or external. When we are continually improving, we often have internal cues of feeling more relaxed, competent and in control. External feedback on our ability to continually improve facets of our life is extremely reinforcing. When I make a speech, give a seminar or workshop, or make a public presentation, I always feel on top of the world and look forward to doing it again. This process is self-reinforcing.

If you work in an environment that promotes CQI, you don't need to look far for a frame-of-reference. However, if one's job culture doesn't promote CQI, a weekly Toastmasters' meeting or any other similar meeting isn't going to make a significant difference in understanding continual improvement. As one increase her participation in any continual improvement effort, the likelihood of internalizing the process increases.

I have observed that some groups have a high success rate with understanding and implementing continual improvement efforts. Successful members of AA, with a few years or more of sobriety, understand maintaining change and have a clear frame-of-reference for this process. The focus of 12-step programs is to enhance one's ability to stay sober or to maintain other desired behaviors. There are many 12-step programs that address multiple issues such as overeating, gambling, and sexual addiction.

Some 12-step program members have found what could be called a 13th step. They have not only maintained change, but they have moved forward to design a life that includes moving forward with purpose and success. However, others continue to smoke, consume unhealthy foods and participate in other risky behavior. The difference between the two levels of outcomes is that, although both groups have the tools for continued improvement, some participants are totally pleased with stopping at sobriety. There is certainly not anything wrong with this.

On an organizational level, CQI is a process of on-going feedback from customers, employees, and others who may be in a position to improve the operation of an organization. Stated another way, it is making informed decisions based on data analysis. Organizations find that this process decreases the number of capricious meetings and gives focus and augments the ability to strategically plan. Feedback from multiple sources enters a feedback loop. The focus on benchmarks diminishes because this self-reinforcing process achieves benchmarks.

On the personal level, you wouldn't focus on losing ten-pounds; you would focus on continually improving your choice of foods and beverages while simultaneously improving your exercise routine. It is true that the goal wouldn't be to continually lose weight, but rather to continually improve one's health. As we age, our bodies begin to deteriorate and our metabolism slows. We lose muscle mass. Thus, if our goal is to continually improve, we will essentially be maintaining our health longer.

For those who don't believe that they have a frame of reference for continual progress, think about how children learn their native language or about how we learn math. These progressions slow with age for most of us, but they continue throughout life. Think about how these processes can be examples of continual improvement during the first few decades of life.

Once adults end formal education, they may have hobbies such as photography, fishing, or playing video games. With the learning of new information, practice, and receiving feedback, we continually improve our level of skill. Give some thought about any adult hobbies that you have where you believe that you are continually improving.

If you look around, you may see that people making continual progress surround you. Much of *Stop the Sabotage* has been written in Barnes and Nobel Cafes. I like to the work in the presence of others. As I write, I look at the array of books and magazines that people bring and leave at the tables. I see those who are learning everything from landscaping design to computer graphics. I hear conversations that lead me to believe that these are on-going interests. Putting ourselves in places where people grow and develop is key to gaining a frame-of-reference for continual progress.

Biographies and autobiographies, whether written or in audio or video format, can give you the inspiration that you need to understand continual improvement. As I stated in Chapter One, don't focus on whether you agree with the person who has continually improved facets of their lives. Focus on their process. Realize that these are people who waste very little time and energy on trivial matters. They have drive and focus.

Carefully examine your life for areas where you have continually improved—areas where you were not thinking about making or maintaining change. For example, if you have been completing crossword puzzles or Sudoku during your commute for the past few years, I assume that you are now more skillful. You can now either go faster or can moved to a more difficult level that requires more skill. The same would be true for playing video games.

Yes, these examples indicate that you have an experiential knowledge of continual improvement. This process is not as foreign as we may think. Once you have identified areas where you have this frame-of-reference for continual improvement and you have made and maintained change for a period of time, you are ready to move forward with intention and purpose.

Keep in mind that your frames-of-reference for maintaining change and for making continual improvement in life may involve very different facets of your life. The key is that you recognize that you have experienced both processes and understand how you achieved both.

Change is about acquiring and about letting go. Hopefully, you have acquired a substantial amount of useful information while reading *Stop the Sabotage*. Focus on identifying and eliminating the personal sabotages that have hindered your ability to make the changes that you desire. Without eliminating or minimizing the effect of your sabotages, you are trying to swim in a lead-filled vest.

The key that unlocks your ability to make and maintain change and then to make continual improvement in life is to recognize your sabotages. Make constant effort to decrease your discounting of information. Realize that the purging of the clutter in your head and the wise and prudent use of your mental time can set you free to a new world of endless possibilities. As you minimize your financing of inane and unproductive action and thought with your energy, your energy increases with clarity and intent.

Use *Stop the Sabotage* as a guide to move forward. Make careful note of your sabotages and work toward eliminating these before moving forward with the contract for change. Without addressing sabotages, you are putting perfume over body odor. At some point, the answer is to take a bath. The process that I have described is a good example of slowing down to move faster. If used thoughtfully, you will not continue to start over multiple times. Go slow and work with intention. Make notes, charts, graphs, or use any other processes that work to personalize this material.

If you use technology, use it as a friend and not as robber of energy, thought, and serenity. I carry my i-Phone and i-Pad with me almost everywhere I go. I record both audio and visual notes, photograph things that assist me with continual improvement and store information that I cross-reference with important aspects of change. If technology isn't your preference, a paper and pen works well. You may want to try, as part of your change and continual improvement process, experimenting with technology to capture your thoughts and images.

Once you have accomplished and maintained your goals, be sure to celebrate your progress and your victories. You will know that your hard work and tenacity has paid off. Gratitude and fear cannot occupy the same space. Know that one of the best ways to maintain your change and to move on to continual improvement is to give it away. When you help others with their growth, you are more likely to stay on the path of continual improvement.

Your progress is up to you. Don't work on yourself in a vacuum. You need to communicate with others who are supportive of you. If you don't have a healthy support system, go slow and reality-test each step along your path. When we stay in our head, we tend to become abstract and lost. Keep it real and keep the focus on you. Develop a plan and stick to it.

I believe in this process because I have worked in public mental health and child welfare for decades. My work as been with people who strive to put together a better life. I sincerely believe in people and their ability to change. Hopefully, *Stop the Sabotage* has assisted in growing your belief in yourself and your ability to make and maintain change. My hope for you is that you will make continual progress throughout life.

About the Author

Herman "Ray" Barber has worked in public mental health and child welfare for over three decades. He has taught college and continuing education courses in both psychology and social work.

Currently he teaches classes in social work ethics, cultural competence, and continuous quality improvement. Ray has presented at numerous national conferences on topics related to improving workforce development through the practice of continual organizational improvement.

As a Commissioner and Team Leader for the Council on Accreditation, he has traveled extensively throughout the country talking with the management, staff, and clients in many types of human service programs. He has found that working with diverse populations throughout the country has kept him grounded in understanding the multitude of problems faced during difficult times.

Ray is a Certified Personal Trainer and Conditioning Specialist and developed a website focusing on continual improvement in life (www.knightsjourney.org) during 2002. His passion is helping others with maintaining personal change and making continual progress in life.

During 2010 he received his DTM (Distinguished Toastmaster) award. He has used the Toastmasters' program to continually improve his public speaking and leadership skills. His two most coveted awards came from services to individuals in need. While serving as a counselor for the U.S. Department of Veterans Affairs, the New River Chapter of Vietnam Veterans of America presented him with a service award. During 2010, Ray's name was added to the Wall of Honor for service to the Carpenter's Shelter in Alexandria, Virginia.

BUY A SHARE OF THE FUTURE IN YOUR COMMUNITY

These certificates make great holiday, graduation and birthday gifts that can be personalized with the recipient's name. The cost of one S.H.A.R.E. or one square foot is $54.17. The personalized certificate is suitable for framing and will state the number of shares purchased and the amount of each share, as well as the recipient's name. The home that you participate in "building" will last for many years and will continue to grow in value.

Here is a sample SHARE certificate:

HABITAT FOR HUMANITY

THIS CERTIFIES THAT

YOUR NAME HERE

HAS INVESTED IN A HOME FOR A DESERVING FAMILY

1985-2010

TWENTY-FIVE YEARS OF BUILDING FUTURES
IN OUR COMMUNITY ONE HOME AT A TIME

1200 SQUARE FOOT HOUSE @ $65,000 = $54.17 PER SQUARE FOOT
This certificate represents a tax deductible donation. It has no cash value.

YES, I WOULD LIKE TO HELP!

I support the work that Habitat for Humanity does and I want to be part of the excitement! As a donor, I will receive periodic updates on your construction activities but, more importantly, I know my gift will help a family in our community realize the dream of homeownership. **I would like to SHARE in your efforts against substandard housing in my community!** *(Please print below)*

PLEASE SEND ME _____ SHARES at $54.17 EACH = $ $_____

In Honor Of: _____

Occasion: (Circle One)   HOLIDAY   BIRTHDAY   ANNIVERSARY

      OTHER: _____

Address of Recipient: _____

Gift From: _____ *Donor Address:* _____

Donor Email: _____

I AM ENCLOSING A CHECK FOR $ $_____ PAYABLE TO HABITAT FOR HUMANITY <u>OR</u> PLEASE CHARGE MY VISA OR MASTERCARD *(CIRCLE ONE)*

Card Number _____ Expiration Date: _____

Name as it appears on Credit Card _____ Charge Amount $ _____

Signature _____

Billing Address _____

Telephone # Day _____ Eve _____

PLEASE NOTE: Your contribution is tax-deductible to the fullest extent allowed by law.
Habitat for Humanity • P.O. Box 1443 • Newport News, VA 23601 • 757-596-5553
www.HelpHabitatforHumanity.org